MW00852138

THE CROSS AND MEDAL OF SAINT

BENEDICT

THE CROSS AND MEDAL OF SAINT

BENEDICT

A MYSTICAL SIGN
OF DIVINE POWER

by

St. Gregory the Great,
Saint Bernard of Clairvaux,
Johannes Trithemius, Pope Benedict XIV,
and others

compiled, translated, and edited by

Fr. Robert Nixon, OSB

TAN Books
Gastonia, North Carolina

Translated by Fr. Robert Nixon, OSB

Cover design by Jordan Avery

Cover image: Saint Peter Martyr with Saints Nicholas and Benedict, 1505-06 (oil on panel), Cima de Congeliano, Giovanni Battista (c. 1459-1517), © Pinacoteca di Brera, Milano / Bridgeman Images

ISBN: 978-1-5051-2284-8
Kindle ISBN: 978-1-5051-2285-5
ePUB ISBN: 978-1-5051-2286-2

Published in the United States by
TAN Books
PO Box 269
Gastonia, NC 28053
www.TANBooks.com

Printed in the United States of America

For the word of the cross,
to them indeed that perish, is foolishness;
but to them that are saved, that is, to us,
it is the power of God.

—1 Corinthians 1:18

CONTENTS

Chronological List of Authors Quoted in This Work

Translation of writings from the various authors listed below (in chronological order of when they lived) form the main substance of this work. All the works from which extracts are taken are in the public domain.

- Pope Saint Gregory the Great
- (Saint) Venantius Fortunatus
- Saint Louis the Pious, Holy Roman Emperor
- Blessed Rabanus Maurus
- Saint Peter Damian
- Saint Anselm of Canterbury
- Saint Bernard of Clairvaux
- Saint Bruno of Segni
- Saint Hildegard of Bingen
- Jacobus de Voragine, Archbishop of Genoa
- Johannes Trithemius, OSB
- Fr. Gabriel Bucelin, OSB
- Abbé Jean-Baptiste Thiers
- Dom Bernhard Pez, OSB

EDITOR'S INTRODUCTION

Saint Benedict of Norcia (480-547) ranks as a towering figure in the ascendency of the Catholic faith in Europe, and in the formation and identity of Western civilization in general. Born to a noble Roman family in the late 5th century, he founded and propelled a monastic movement which was destined to change history forever. This movement, which began with a single young man, Benedict of Norcia, responding to the call of God, went on to become the dominant spiritual and cultural force in Western Europe throughout the entire Middle Ages. It was this monastic movement which brought the Catholic faith to the furthermost reaches of the West and even to the world beyond. And it was not only the Catholic faith which it propagated, but culture, learning, and civilization as an integrated totality. Indeed, it is fitting that Saint Benedict is revered as the Patron of Europe, for his influence permeates all aspects of both the Western Church and our Western culture.

Throughout the Middle Ages, Benedictine monasteries functioned as the primary repositories of knowledge, centers of learning, orphanages, hospitals, and guardians of religious orthodoxy and civil order. The number of saints whom this noble order has produced is virtually beyond number. In the 14th century, a list was made of recognized Benedictine saints and included over 15,000 individuals. Moreover, the Order of Saint Benedict is the most ancient religious order within the Catholic Church, predating all others by many centuries.

Saint Benedict continues to be recognized and revered by the faithful as an inspiring example of humility, courage, and fidelity, and continues to be invoked as a powerful and efficacious intercessor and spiritual guide. The Rule of Saint Benedict, which has served to direct and govern the lives of literally millions of monks and nuns over the centuries, presents a prudent, sustainable, and healthy balance of prayer and work. This balance is reflected in the popular saying: *Ora et labora* ("Pray and work"). But the official motto of the Order of Saint Benedict is perhaps even more illuminating as to this balance, and to its final purpose: *Ut in omnibus glorificetur Deus* ("May God be glorified in all things"). This expresses the notion that all activities of life (including formal prayer, contemplation, work, and even rest and recreation) should be dedicated to the glory of God. And this is no less true for lay Catholics than it is for monks and nuns.

An important element in the popular devotion to this great saint is the medal or cross which is associated with him, and which is the particular focus of this publication. The medal or cross of Saint Benedict has been found by countless people in our own age to be of great benefit and potency, and the number of its devotees, as well as the depth of interest in it, seems to be ever increasing. But the history and true meaning of this venerable and potent sacred sigil[1] are known (at least with accuracy, certainty, and completeness) by very few.

This present volume aims to correct this lacuna.[2] Drawing upon a variety of authentic and reliable sources, the full story of the history, meaning, and potency of the medal will be explained in the following pages. Firstly, the life and legend of Saint Benedict himself, together with the miraculous and rapid progress of the order he founded, are included, taken from the most ancient and reliable authorities. Of course, to write a comprehensive history of Benedictine monasticism would be almost as difficult as writing a comprehensive history of European civilization or the Church itself. Nevertheless, the details provided here form a very solid and (it is hoped) sufficient overview. This background knowledge on the Benedictine tradition, which manifests the vital importance of Saint Benedict as the Patriarch of Western Monasticism in the history of the Catholic Church, is an important pre-condition for proper appreciation of, and access to, the immense power of his medal.

Following this, the design of the medal will be described and illustrated, with the hidden meaning of its various elements clearly and carefully explained.

Then, drawing upon Fr. Gabriel Bucelin's monumental and magisterial volume *Benedictus Redivivus*[3] (1679) and other early sources, the remarkable story of how the power,

---

[1]   Symbol or seal.
[2]   Missing part or gap.
[3]   Benedict Revived.

efficacy, and significance of the medal came to be generally known to the Catholic faithful will be revealed. This fascinating series of events involves the arrest and exposure of a coven of wizards and the chance discovery of an ancient manuscript in a Bavarian monastery which solved the riddle of the meaning of the letters inscribed on the medal. A selection of the countless miracles reliably attributed to the power of this mystical sigil will also be offered, again from authentic early sources.

Finally, a translation of the papal brief of approval of the medal or cross from the Holy See, issued by Pope Benedict XIV in 1741, is given. This document includes also the approved form of blessing for the medal, and the indulgences extended to those who wear it.

It is hoped that this modest but important work will promote devotion to our Holy Father, Saint Benedict, the Patron of Europe and the Patriarch of All Monks of the West. Through the medal or cross of Saint Benedict, may he continue to guide and protect all those who venerate him and who strive to serve faithfully the same Master whom he served with such singular fidelity, humility, courage, and wisdom—Our Lord Jesus Christ, to whom be glory forever and ever. Amen.

Sancte Benedicte, ora pro nobis!
Fr. Robert Nixon, OSB
Abbey of the Most Holy Trinity
New Norcia, Western Australia

Chapter 1

The Saints Praise Saint Benedict and His Holy Rule

1.
Saint Gregory the Great
(From Book II of His Dialogues)

The man of God, Saint Benedict, shone in this world with a multitude of miracles and was no less radiant by virtue of his eloquence and wisdom. For he wrote a rule for monks distinguished by its discretion, and most lucid in its wording. If anyone wishes to know in more detail the life and habits of this saint, he is able to find them portrayed in his Holy Rule. For the holy man was utterly incapable of teaching anything which he himself did not first fulfill perfectly in his own manner of living.

2.
SAINT LOUIS THE PIOUS, HOLY ROMAN EMPEROR
(FROM HIS EXHORTATION OF EIGEL, ABBOT OF FULDA)

The Rule of Saint Benedict is indeed the "narrow gate" which leads all those who follow it to God! For it will teach you everything you need to know of discretion, good measure, and charity.

3.
SAINT PETER DAMIAN
(FROM HIS OPUSCULUM XIII)

The Holy Rule of Saint Benedict is like a spacious and beautiful mansion! For it is capable of accommodating individuals of each and every type, and leading them to the perfection and summit of sanctity—both the young and the old, the strong and the weak, and the learned and the simple alike.

4.
SAINT ANSELM OF CANTERBURY
(FROM HIS PRAYER TO SAINT BENEDICT)

O holy and blessed Benedict! You were enriched with such a vast treasury of celestial grace that it drew not only you to the very heights of glory, to eternal peace, and to the throne of heaven—but also led innumerable multitudes of other souls to the same blessedness. You drew them in by your admirable and noble manner of life; you inspired them with your persuasive encouragement; you instructed them with your wise teaching; and, finally, you astonished them with your countless miracles!

Flying to you, O Saint Benedict, I prostrate my weak and sorely troubled soul before you. To you I pour out my humble prayers. For by my vows and by my monastic habit, I have committed myself to the monastic life; yet I recognize that I very often stray far from the high ideals of this commitment!

Be with me, therefore, O Holy Father Benedict, as I beseech your help. You are the most illustrious general among the many leaders of the army of Christ, and I am sworn to you as my commander, though I am but an incompetent soldier. Raise me up when I fall, grant me victory, and finally lead me to the crown of triumph; so that, under your guidance, we may rejoice with you in the presence of our eternal King, who lives and reigns forever and ever! Amen.

5.
SAINT BERNARD OF CLAIRVAUX (FROM HIS SERMON ON THE FEAST DAY OF SAINT BENEDICT)

Today, we celebrate the feast day of our glorious master, Saint Benedict! His most sweet name is to be embraced and honored by you, brethren, with all joy; for he is our leader, our teacher, and our law-giver. I constantly delight in his memory, although I may scarcely dare to recall the name of our Blessed Father without feelings of my own inadequacy and unworthiness. Brothers, like you all, I am called to renunciation of the vanities of this passing world and to humble and obedient acceptance of monastic discipline. But, unlike you, I am called to share with Benedict the title and position of "Abbot." He bore that title, and truly and worthily; whereas I am a mere shadow of what an abbot should be and what he actually was!

Saint Benedict was like a great tree of stupendous size and filled with a magnificent abundance of fruit—indeed, like the tree mentioned in the psalm, which is "planted by the flowing waters."[4] But where is it, you may ask, that waters typically flow? It is in the shaded depths of valleys, in between the mountain peaks. For we have all perceived that streams of water flow down the mountain slopes to form a river in the depth of a valley below. Thus it is that in the lowliness of humility, rather than on the peaks of pride, the crystalline rivers of grace flow most copiously. O, all you who wish to be faithful beasts in the service of the sweet yoke of Christ and to live as sheep in His flock, gather in this verdant valley of humility, where your teacher Saint Benedict once stood before you! For the peaks of the mountains of pride are barren, rocky and perilous, populated by deadly vipers, and devoid of pasture. But in the shaded glens of humility's valley, there shall you find serene meadows and quiet waters aplenty. And

---

[4]   Psalms 1:3.

there it was that Benedict was firmly planted—the noble tree, nourished by the waters of heavenly grace, who produced the wonderful fruit of innumerable saints throughout the ages.

6.
SAINT BRUNO, BISHOP OF SEGNI
(FROM HIS BOOKS OF SENTENCES)

What shall I say of the blessed Saint Benedict? In writing his Holy Rule, he has opened up a well from which sweet and healing waters flow forth. These waters of sanctity and wisdom satisfy the thirsting souls which drink from them. After the Apostles and the Evangelists, no other saint has satisfied the spiritual thirst of so many people, and liberated so many souls from the peril of death and the tyranny of the passions!

7.
SAINT HILDEGARD OF BINGEN
(FROM HER COMMENTARY ON
THE RULE OF SAINT BENEDICT)

Our Holy Father, Saint Benedict, wrote his Rule in fear of God and piety, graced with perfect charity and perfect chastity. Therefore nothing should be taken away from, nor added to, his wise teaching. For there is nothing lacking in them, nor is there anything superfluous. For, indeed, when the saint composed his rule, it was the Holy Spirit Himself that was guiding him.

CHAPTER 2

THE LIFE AND MIRACLES OF SAINT BENEDICT

adapted from
Book II of the Dialogues *of Saint Gregory the Great*

Editor's note: *The earliest and most authoritative biography of Saint Benedict was written by Saint Gregory the Great. Saint Gregory, who served as pope from 590-604, was believed to have been a close relative of Saint Benedict, both saints being members of the noble Anicius family. Before being elected to the papacy, Gregory had founded some three monasteries in Rome, all of which followed the Rule of Saint Benedict, and he lived as a monk in one of these for several years. While pope, he often expressed a longing for the opportunities for solitude and contemplation which monastic life had afforded him.*

His biography of Saint Benedict forms Book II of his Dialogues. *The present life closely follows that given in this source, but (for the sake of brevity and clarity) it has been adapted to take the form of a continuous narrative, rather than a dialogue. This adaptation draws also upon the life of Benedict found in the* Golden Legend, *compiled in the 13th century by Jacobus de Voragine, which is itself closely modeled on Gregory's version.*

*　　　＊ ＊ ＊*

There was a man of venerable life, blessed both by grace and by name, for he was called "Benedict," which means "Blessed." From his youthful years, he always had the maturity of an old man; for his virtue far surpassed his age. He withheld his soul from all vain pleasures. And though he was in the world and, because of his wealth and status, might freely have enjoyed everything that it offers, he looked upon it all with complete detachment. Indeed, he regarded the world and its allurements as a barren desert.

I have not been able to ascertain all the noteworthy deeds and events of his life; but those few, which I shall now describe to you, I have learned by the word-of-mouth testimony of four of his disciples, who knew him personally and witnessed these things for themselves.

Benedict was born in the province of Norcia,[5] and from there was sent to Rome to pursue a liberal education, according to the usual custom. But whilst still a child, he abandoned his literary studies and resolved to seek solitude in

---

[5]   Norcia is approximately one hundred miles north-east of Rome. According to other sources, Benedict was born to the noble Anicius family, and was thus related to Boethius, Saint Gregory the Great, Pope Felix III, and many other illustrious personages. His father was Eupropius and his mother was Abundantia.

order to lead a life of contemplation and prayer. He therefore went forth alone, accompanied only by his nurse (who loved him dearly), and arrived at a place called Affile.[6]

Having arrived there, his nurse obtained a sieve with which to winnow wheat. But she happened to place this sieve on a table somewhat carelessly, and it fell to the floor and broke cleanly into two parts. Benedict saw his nurse weeping over this accident and was at once moved to pity towards her. Taking the fractured sieve, the holy boy prayed over it intently. And, lo, it was restored to perfect completeness in the twinkling of an eye, as if it had never been damaged!

A little later, Benedict secretly fled from his nurse and went off completely alone. He arrived at a certain place and remained there for three years. This place was located by the side of a pleasant lake, and so is known as "*Sub Lacu*." [7] During this period he had no human contact, with the single exception of a monk by the name of Romanus. This holy Romanus sedulously provided Benedict with all the necessities of life.

---

[6]   According to other sources, Benedict was fourteen years of age when he left Rome to pursue the eremitic life. The name of his nurse was Cyrilla. Some sources indicate that Benedict's mother died while he was still an infant (or even in childbirth), and that Cyrilla had nursed and raised him (together with Scholastica) in place of his mother. According to Gregory's version of his life, whilst at Affile (a location about thirty miles east of Rome) he took up residence in a church dedicated to Saint Peter.

[7]   This name means "beside [or below] a lake." The current Italian form of the name of the place is Subiaco. The monastery at Subiaco is referred to in the Benedictine Order as the "proto-monastery," as it was the very first community which Benedict led.

Now, Benedict dwelt in a deep cave which was not possible for Romanus himself to reach. So it was his practice to attach a basket containing bread to a rope and to lower it to the hermit. He also attached a small bell to the rope, so that the man of God would hear its tinkling and know when supplies were being lowered to him. But the devil, the ancient enemy, was filled with envy at both the charity of Romanus and the refreshment and sustenance being received by Benedict. So the arch-fiend maliciously hurled a stone at the bell and shattered it to pieces! Nevertheless, the diligent Romanus refused to be deterred or frightened by this, and continued to supply the holy hermit with his needs.

Some time afterwards, the Lord appeared to a certain priest who was preparing a festive meal for himself to celebrate Easter. And God said to him, "Here you are, preparing a feast of fine delicacies for your own consumption, while my servant, Benedict, is tormented by hunger!" Upon hearing this, the priest was filled with compunction. He arose and went off to find the saint, taking the food with him. Eventually (and with some difficulty), he located him and said, "Arise, my brother! Let us eat together, for this is the day of Easter."

To this Benedict replied, "Truly, I now know that it is Easter, for I have received the singular blessing of your visit!" Indeed, at that time, the saint was leading an isolated life and had no other way in which he could have known that it was Easter on that day. The priest said to him, "Since it is now the feast of the Lord's Resurrection, it does not behoove us to be sparing with food or drink! Therefore I have come to you so that we may celebrate together." And, blessing God, the hermit and the priest enjoyed a fine Easter banquet that day.

* * *

One day as Benedict was out walking, a certain species of black bird, known as a "merle," began to fly around his face in a most annoying manner. And so persistently and closely did the bird plague him that he would have been able to capture it in his hand, had he so wished. But instead, the saint simply made the sign of the cross, and at once, the bird departed from him.

The devil then tempted him in another form, by drawing before the eyes of his mind the image of a certain very attractive woman whom he had previously seen. This ignited such a flame of desire in the heart of the hermit that he seriously considered departing from the solitude and abandoning his life of prayer and contemplation altogether. But suddenly, thanks to the intervention of divine grace, he returned to his better senses and recalled his earnest vows and intentions. Then he threw himself into some nettle bushes which were close at hand, and he rolled himself back and forth vigorously. The wounds which he suffered thereby on his body served to cure the wound of fleshly temptation which had afflicted his mind, and the smarting sting of the thorns upon his skin served to extinguish the burning flame of lust in his heart. And from that time, Benedict was never again tempted by carnal desires or concupiscence of the flesh.

✷ ✷ ✷

Benedict's renown for wisdom and sanctity became ever greater as time went by. Now it happened that the abbot of a certain nearby monastery passed away. And the entire community of monks there then went to Benedict and implored him to lead them as their new abbot. For a long time, he was very reluctant to agree to this proposal, saying that his own manner of life and theirs did not accord at all well. But at last, he was overcome by their entreaties and supplications, and he consented to become their abbot.

Having assumed this position, Benedict very soon perceived that they did not observe many of the proper rules of monastic life, and he duly reproved them for their shortcomings with paternal care. But as a result of this, many of the monks began to regret that they had asked Benedict to lead them, for they realized that their dissipated way of life would not be tolerated by the saint. When they saw that what they had previously been accustomed to do freely was now no longer permitted to them, they resolved to rid themselves of their new abbot, by fair means or foul. So some of them secretly mixed some poison in with wine. This they brought to Benedict as he was seated at the table. But he made the sign of the cross over it, and at once the glass goblet which contained the wine shattered, as if it had been struck by a rock! He then realized that the wine had been poisoned—that it was indeed a cup of death, since it was not able to withstand or resist the cross, which is the sign of eternal life.

The saint then arose and, with a placid and serene face, said, "May almighty God have mercy on you, brethren! Did I not tell you that your manner of life and my own would not accord?" Having said this, he departed from the community and returned to his beloved solitude to resume his former eremitic life. But his fame continued steadily to increase, and his sanctity was plainly demonstrated by a multitude of signs and miracles. A vast number of people visited him, and many wished to join him in living the monastic life. And so within a short time, he had founded no less than twelve monasteries.

✳ ✳ ✳

In one of these monasteries, there was a certain monk who found himself unable to stand still in prayer for any length of time. Rather, while the others were praying, he would leave the oratory and go and wander about outside. When the abbot of that monastery related this troubling thing to Saint Benedict, he visited the monastery for himself, and saw the monk who was unable to remain still in prayer. And he noticed a small boy vexing the monk, pushing him about in a persistent fashion and drawing him to-and-fro by the cloth of his habit. Benedict was surprised at this uncanny thing and said to the abbot and another monk, Maur, "Do you not see the troublesome boy that is preventing this poor monk from standing still and causing him to wander around?" But both of them, perplexed, declared that they could see no such thing.

The saint then invited them to pray with him, that they should be able to see the cause of the monk's strange behavior. And, behold, the eyes of Maur were opened, and he perceived the small, impish boy. But the abbot of the monastery could still not see him.

The next day, Benedict found this monk outside wandering around aimlessly when he should have been in the oratory in prayer. With a certain degree of paternal severity and charitable discipline, he reprimanded him for his lack of wisdom and discernment and struck him with his staff. At this, the monk fell down motionless. And after that, the devil—for it was, in fact, the devil who had assumed the form of this vexatious child—never troubled him again. It was as if the staff of Benedict had not struck the hapless monk, but rather driven away the wicked tempter himself!

* * *

Out of the dozen monasteries which Benedict founded, there were three which were located on the top of a rocky mountain. And each day, some monks of these communities would have to perform the laborious task of descending from the mountain, drawing water, and carrying their burden back up to the mountain peaks. They often requested that Benedict would permit them to relocate their communities, so that they might be spared this arduous necessity.

So, one night, Benedict ascended the mountain, taking a young monk with him. There they prayed earnestly to God, and the saint positioned three large stones to identify a particular location amongst the mountainous peaks. The next morning, some of the brothers came to Benedict once more. This time, he said to them, "My sons, go to the very peak of the mountain, and on it you will find three large stones carefully positioned. At the spot marked by these stones, dig into the ground. And you will find that the Lord is able to produce for you all the water you need!"

So, the brethren ascended the mountain and found the place where the three stones had been positioned. They began to dig in the place thus indicated, and suddenly crystal-clear water flowed forth! This water flowed continuously, forming a stream running from the peak of the mountain to its base. And this miraculous spring was sufficient to provide the monks with all the water they needed and to spare them the irksome necessity of the daily trek down the mountain to visit the well.

✳ ✳ ✳

In a certain place near one of Saint Benedict's monasteries, one of the monks was engaged in clearing an area of land from the profusion of thornbushes and brambles which infested it. He was using an axe to do this, and it happened that the iron head of the axe he was using flew off the handle (such indeed was the vigor of his exertions!) and landed in a nearby pond. This pond was extremely deep, and the sunken axe head seemed to be irretrievably lost. The monk was, as may be imagined, overcome with anxiety and sorrow. But upon learning of this accident, blessed Benedict confidently took the handle of the axe and held it over the surface of the water. And immediately, the axe head sprung up from the depths of the pond and re-affixed itself to the handle!

* * *

One of Saint Benedict's young disciples in the monastic life, a boy called Placid,[8] was once drawing water from a certain great river. Alas, while thus engaged, the unfortunate neophyte slipped and fell into the deep and turbulent waters! Instantly, the waves engulfed him and drew him out into the depths until he was the distance of an arrow-shot from the bank. Saint Benedict, the man of God, was back at the monastery in his cell when this occurred, but, through a spirit of prophecy, he knew immediately what had happened. At once, he summoned another monk, Maur,[9] and related to

---

[8] According to ancient traditions, Placid was eight years of age when he joined Saint Benedict's monastery. Like Benedict, he was of the illustrious Anicius family. A Saint Placid (believed to be this same disciple of Benedict) is revered as a martyr in Sicily, where he founded a monastery. This monastery was attacked by Saracens and he, together with thirty other monks, were all slaughtered. See Usuard's *Martyrologium,* October 5.

[9] Saint Maur and Saint Placid, the two disciples of Benedict mentioned by name in his life, entered monastic life on the same day in the year 523. According to tradition, Saint Maur was sent to France by Saint Benedict in 543, at the request of Innocentius, the bishop of Le Mans. He founded the first Benedictine monastery in France and served as its abbot, in a location now called Saint Maur-sur-Loire.

him what had occurred, bidding him to set forth with all haste to rescue Placid from drowning. Having received a quick blessing from the saint, Maur rushed forth to the place where Placid had been drawing water. And so intent was he upon rescuing the lad that he did not halt even when he had arrived at the bank of the river, but continued running over the water just as if he was still running on the land! He found Placid, and grasping him by the hair, drew him forth from the waves and back to safety.

It was only after the rescue was complete that Maur realized the marvelous thing which had taken place. When he recounted it to Benedict, the saint humbly insisted that the miracle was not due to his own (Benedict's) merits or sanctity, but rather entirely attributable to the diligent and praiseworthy obedience of Maur himself.

* * *

There was a certain priest by the name of Florentius who became inflamed with envy at Benedict's reputation for holiness, and this envy soon grew into wicked malice. So Florentius took a loaf of bread, soaked it in poison, and then took it to Benedict, pretending that he wished the saint to bless it for him and to accept it as a gift. Benedict took the bread gratefully, but sensing by prophetic insight that it was poisoned, gave it to a raven which he was in the habit of feeding. And he spoke to the bird thus, "In the name of the Lord Jesus Christ, take this bread to some place where no human shall ever find it!"

The raven then flew around the bread crowing vociferously, as if wishing to obey Benedict's instructions but somehow unable to do so. The man of God then repeated his words, "I say to thee, my feathered friend, take thou this bread and hie thee hence with it! Then cast it away in some deserted place." Upon hearing this, the raven did exactly as it had been asked. After three days, the sable-plumed fowl returned to the saint to resume its wonted custom of accepting daily a little food from his venerable hand.

But despite the frustration of this attempted poisoning, the nefarious Florentius did not immediately cease his plotting against Benedict. For perceiving that he was unable to harm the body of the master, he resolved instead to attack the souls of his disciples. So he engaged seven beautiful maidens, and he would pay them to go to the garden of the monastery and to play and dance there, quite naked.[10] It was, indeed, his scheme to incite thereby the young monks to thoughts of fornication and to inflame their hearts with the distracting and insidious fires of carnal lust.

When Benedict saw what was taking place and how Florentius was working to corrupt his community, he resolved to depart to another locality, together with his brethren monks. Now, the dastardly Florentius was looking on as all of this was happening, sitting in a chamber at the top of a

---

[10] It is not entirely clear whether the sending of these seductive dancers to the monastery was a once-off incident, or whether it was a regular practice of Florentius to do so. Benedict's decision to relocate the community seems to suggest the latter.

solarium (or sun-tower). And he rejoiced with a most wicked joy. Yet suddenly, the solarium collapsed, and the envious cleric fell to his death!

Maur, who had remained behind and witnessed this, rushed after Benedict and the monks who were traveling with him. With great exultation, he said to him, "O master, the one who has been seeking to undermine you is now dead!" But the saint did not rejoice when he heard this, as one may well have expected him to do; but, on the contrary, he wept bitterly. Perhaps he wept to hear of the demise the Florentius himself; or perhaps he mourned that his disciple, Maur, should exult thus over the death of his foe.

Wisely, then, did Benedict enjoin Maur to repentance over his presumptuous exultation at the death of another human being. He also declared that, though one may change the location where one resides, nevertheless the real enemy—that is the devil—will work the same temptations in every place.

* * *

In due course, Benedict moved to Monte Cassino and established a monastery there. He transformed an ancient temple of Apollo to a chapel dedicated to Saint John the Baptist, and also converted the people of the area away from the practice of idolatry to the Christian faith.

This so infuriated the devil that he appeared before the eyes of the saint in a visible and most gruesome form, with acrid flames spewing forth from his eyes and mouth. He called upon the saint, saying "O Benedict! Benedict!" But when Benedict utterly ignored him and refused to respond, he cried out instead, "I should not call thee 'Benedict,' for that means 'blessed.' Rather I should dub thee, 'Accursed, accursed!' Why is it that thou doth persecute me thus?"[11]

* * *

When the monastery at Monte Cassino was being constructed, there was a large boulder which the monks needed to move for the purpose of their building work there. Yet, try as they might, they could not manage to budge the boulder, even when working together as a large group. But when the saint gave his blessing over the immense stone, instantly the boulder was moved without any effort at all! Reflecting upon this, he realized that it had been the devil himself who, until then, had been preventing them from shifting the boulder.

Another time, still in the days of the construction of the abbey at Monte Cassino, the monks were at work raising up a wall. The devil again appeared to Benedict and said to him maliciously, "I shall go off now to vex your beloved brethren!" But the saint hastily sent a message to the monks, urging them to exercise all possible caution because the malign and cunning devil was intent upon causing them trouble.

Nevertheless, the devil did succeed in pushing the new wall over, and it fell upon a certain monk and crushed him to death. When the holy abbot heard of this, he ordered that

---

[11] See Acts 9:4.

the body of the unfortunate brother be placed in a sack and brought to him anon.[12] This was done, and Saint Benedict prayed over him. And, lo, the dead monk was instantly restored to full life and health!

* * *

There was a certain devout layman, who had a custom of visiting Saint Benedict at his monastery once every year. And it was his practice to fast whilst making the journey there. But one year, another pilgrim joined him in his travels. This pilgrim had some food with him. Once evening had fallen, he said to his companion, "Come, brother, let us eat together, lest we lose strength for our journey." But the other explained that it was his intention to fast until he had completed his pilgrimage to visit the saint.

For the moment, his companion accepted his declining to share food with him with apparent good grace. But a little later, he asked him again to eat with him. And again, his companion politely refused. After they had traveled further and were both much fatigued, they came upon a cool fountain. The unknown pilgrim once more suggested to his companion that they should partake of the refreshment of a little food and drink. This time, his companion gave in, and they ate together.

When the man finally reached the monastery at Monte Cassino, he was taken into the presence of Saint Benedict.

---

[12] At once, immediately.

The saint looked upon him intently and said, "My son, the wicked devil tried to tempt you once and was not able to succeed. Then he tried to tempt you a second time, and you successfully refused him. But when he tempted you for the third time, you were defeated!" Upon hearing this, the pilgrim realized that his mysterious traveling companion had, in fact, been the Prince of Darkness himself. Overcome with remorse, he fell at the feet of the holy abbot and implored his prayers.

* * *

Attila, the King of the Goths, wished to test whether or not Saint Benedict really possessed the spirit of prophecy, as he was reputed to do. So, he had a certain one of his officers dressed in his own royal robes and gave to him all the regalia and adornments of a king. He then sent him forth to the monastery, instructing the officer to pretend to be himself. But as soon as Benedict glanced at him, he saw through the attempted impersonation and said, "My son, discard this foolish disguise! For I perceive clearly that the costume you wear and the regalia that adorns your person is not, in sooth,[13] your own at all."

And immediately, the officer fell to the ground, struck with awe and reverence, and he was deeply sorry that he had presumed to attempt to deceive such a sagacious and holy man.

* * *

---

[13] Truth.

There was a certain cleric who was greatly vexed by a devil, and he was taken to Saint Benedict in the hope that the man of God might be able to cure him of this affliction. The saint duly performed an exorcism. Once the man had been freed from the evil spirit that had hitherto vexed him, Benedict instructed him, "My son, henceforth eat no meat. And neither should you ever accept sacramental ordination to the priesthood. For if you are ever ordained as a priest, you will once more be delivered into the power of the wicked one!"

For a good while, the cleric carefully observed Benedict's injunctions. But as he saw many of his juniors being advanced to the priesthood, he became frustrated and envious. Eventually, casting Benedict's earnest warning to the desuetude[14] of oblivion, he accepted the advancement which he felt was due to him and was ordained as a priest. And from that time forth, the devil did indeed begin to vex and afflict him once more . . .

* * *

Once , a certain man sent two flagons of wine to Saint Benedict through a servant of his. But this dishonest thrall hid one of the flagons along the way and delivered only the other one. The man of God accepted this gift with expressions of gratitude. But—illuminated by the vision of prophecy which revealed to him the covert actions of all—he said to the servant, "My son, see to it that you don't drink from the other flagon,

---

[14] Discontinuance from use or exercise.

the one you have secretly hidden away for yourself! Rather, inspect it most cautiously to see what peril lurks therein!"

The servant was, naturally, deeply embarrassed and confused by this exposure of his own deceitfulness and attempted theft. Bearing in mind the words of the saint, when he came to the flagon which he had hidden, he looked inside cautiously. And there he found lurking within a deadly viper!

* * *

There was a son of an illustrious and wealthy nobleman who had joined Benedict's monastery as a monk. On one occasion, he was assigned the duty of holding the lamp while Benedict ate his dinner. Alas, feelings of pride began to flare up in the young man's heart, and he secretly mused to himself, "Who am I that I should be reduced to standing here holding a lamp for this pitiful old man to eat his repast?"

As he was thinking thus, immediately the saint said to him, "Cross your heart, my son, cross your heart!" And, showing that he was capable of perceiving clearly the innermost sentiments of anyone's soul, he continued thus;

> "O, why, my son, doth there abide
> Within thy heart such wicked pride?
> Why despise, O haughty brother,
> The Love which bids us serve each other?"

And having said this, Benedict summoned another one of the brethren to himself and handed him the lamp to hold. As for the proud monk, he gently directed him to go back to his cell and to reflect quietly on the sin of pride to which he had so easily succumbed . . .

* * *

There was a certain chieftain of the Goths by the name of Galla, who was a member of the sect of the Arians.[15] Galla lived during the time of the aforementioned King Attila, and he persecuted religious persons and the Catholic Church with a baleful ardor. Indeed, he once boasted that any cleric or monk who dared to appear before his face would not depart from him alive.

One day, goaded on by avarice, he captured a farmer and demanded of him all his money and treasures, beating the poor man mercilessly. But the farmer told him (quite truthfully) that he had given everything he possessed that was of value to Saint Benedict and had commended it all to his safe keeping. Upon hearing this, Galla ceased to beat him, but tied him by his arm to the bridle of his horse. He then compelled the farmer to lead him forth, so as to show him who this Benedict was and where he abided.

Thus, the farmer led the brutal Goth to the saint's monastery. With the farmer still leading him, eventually Galla found Benedict, who was sitting alone in his cell and reading. The farmer said, "This is the holy Benedict of whom I

---

[15] The Arians were a heterodox Christian sect, who did not accept the consubstantiality of the Son and the Father, as affirmed in the Niceno-Constantinopolitan creed. At the time of Benedict, many of the Goths and other Germanic peoples still followed this sect.

spoke before." The barbarian was filled with fury and greed, and he demanded of Benedict that he should at once hand over to him the money and treasures which the farmer had entrusted to him.

Upon hearing this, the saint raised his eyes and looked at both Galla and the captured farmer intently. He then turned his gaze to the ropes with which the farmer was bound. And at once, these ropes began to unbind themselves with a rapidity surpassing that which any human being could possibly achieve! The Goth was astounded and fell to the ground in awe, commending himself to the prayers and mercy of the man of God, who could unbind strong ropes with a mere glance.

But Benedict continued his reading casually, barely raising his eyes from the book with which he was engaged. Finally, however, he warned the chieftain of the Goths to abandon his career of brutality, cruelty and tyranny. And henceforth, Galla never again engaged in the crimes of rapine, theft, or intimidation, nor did he make any further efforts to oppress or persecute Catholics.

* * *

At one time, a dire famine struck the Italian region of Campania. Lack of food afflicted the whole population, and even Saint Benedict's monastery was totally bereft of supplies of grain. Their stores of bread were eventually so depleted that once when it was time for all the brethren to take their dinner, only five loaves could be found. When the holy abbot saw the monks looking dejected and depressed at this, he gently admonished them, saying, "Why are your hearts saddened by this lack of bread? Today we have little; but, by the grace of God, tomorrow we shall have an abundance!"

And it happened that, on the morn of the following day, some two hundred sacks filled with flour were discovered outside the cellar door! This was certainly the gracious gift of almighty God, but even to this day it remains an utter mystery as to how they came to be there . . .

When the brethren saw this wonder, they all gave heartfelt thanks to the Lord. Moreover, they learnt the valuable lesson that the generosity of Divine Providence is never to be doubted.

* * *

Once, St. Benedict sent a group of monks to a certain location to construct a new monastery there. He also advised them that he would come to them on a particular day, in order to instruct them concerning the planning and arrangements of the new establishment. Now, on the night before he was due to visit them, he appeared in a dream to the monk who was in charge of the construction party. In this dream, he carefully indicated to that monk his desired layout for the monastery and where the various buildings should be located.

But the next day, when this monk related his vision to the other monks, they all refused to put any trust or credence in the dream. And they were disappointed when Benedict did not appear in person, as he had promised them. So they all went back to the saint and complained to him, "We waited for you patiently to come as you promised, Father Benedict. But you never arrived!"

The man of God responded, "Why ever do you say these things? Did I not appear to one of you in a dream, and clearly indicate how the monastery was to be arranged? Go forth, my sons, and complete the project just as I have instructed you." And having spoken thus, he dismissed the brothers to return to the site of their work and continue their assigned task there.

* * *

Not far from Benedict's monastery, there was a convent of religious sisters. Within this community of nuns, there were two noblewomen who were both highly talkative and not at all able to restrain their tongues from gossip and chatter. Understandably, this undisciplined talk often provoked the superior of the community to anger and annoyance. So, the superior related this problem to Saint Benedict. He, in turn, sent a firm message to the talkative sisters, "Learn to restrain your speech, my sisters, or I shall have no choice but to exclude you both from holy communion!"

Yet, for various reasons, the superior did not pass this message on to them immediately. And, in just a few days, both of the talkative sisters died! Alas, neither of them had received Benedict's instruction on learning to restrain their speech before departing from this passing world. Following their deaths, according to custom, they were both duly buried in the church of the convent.

Now it happened soon afterwards that when Mass was being celebrated in that church, the deacon, pursuant to the usual ritual of the Mass, pronounced the instruction, "Whoever is not able to receive communion should now depart from the church." And, lo, the maidservant of the two deceased noblewomen saw them both arise from their tombs, stand up, and walk out of the church!

Greatly disturbed by this, she reported her vision to Saint Benedict. Upon hearing what she had seen, the saint gave to her an offering to present on behalf of the dead women, saying, "Go and offer this for their deceased souls, and then they shall no longer be excluded from communion, but gladly re-admitted!" This the maidservant did, presenting the offering Benedict had given her on behalf of the two women. And the next time Mass was celebrated in the church, she no longer saw the vision of the deceased nuns arising from their tombs to leave.

* * *

Once, a monk of Saint Benedict's monastery went to visit his parents, but he departed from the monastery without first receiving the saint's blessing. And it happened, alas, that on the very day he arrived to see them, he suddenly died.

But when they attempted to bury their deceased son, the ground opened up and rejected his body! This happened not only once, but a second and even a third time. The parents, greatly distressed, then went to see Benedict, and implored his blessing for their deceased son. The saint took a consecrated eucharistic host and handed it to them, saying "Place this upon his chest, and then lower him into the grave." The parents did this just as the holy abbot had instructed, and this time the body was accepted by the earth and buried successfully.

* * *

There was another monk who, for various reasons, felt himself no longer able to remain in the monastery. He persistently requested of Benedict permission to depart from the community; and eventually, the saint, much irritated and disappointed, granted him leave to do so.

But as he made his way from the monastery, he soon encountered a fierce dragon, standing before him on the road. The beast leered at him with gaping, voracious jaws and fetid, foul, and fiery breath, and seemed fully intent upon devouring him. Aghast with fear, the horrified monk called out, "My brethren, run! Hasten hither and save my life, for this dragon is about to kill me!"

The brothers heard his cries, and they ran out to help him with all possible celerity. But they found no dragon there at all—just the monk, who was crouching and trembling with abject terror. They led him back to the monastery, and he promised henceforth never to attempt to leave again.

* * *

There was another time when a severe famine again afflicted the region. During this time, Saint Benedict would distribute all food and produce that was available to him to those who were destitute. Thus it came about that all the stores of the monastery were becoming drastically depleted, until nothing remained but a glass bottle filled with oil. And then the saint instructed the monk in charge of the cellar to give this one last bottle of oil to a certain needy person.

The cellarer heard this instruction, but he refused to obey it, lest the monks in the monastery should have nothing at all. When the man of God heard of this, he was infuriated. He ordered that the glass bottle of oil should be thrown out the window, so that no trace of disobedience should remain in the monastery.

This was done, and the glass vessel fell heavily upon a great rock on the ground below. But amazingly, it was not broken, nor was a single drop of oil spilt! Saint Benedict then ordered it to be taken up again and given to the needy person, just as he had first instructed.

The cellarer then sincerely reproved himself for his insubordination and lack of confidence in Divine Providence, praying earnestly to God for forgiveness. Now, there was a large stone flask in the monastery that had stood empty for some time. But after the remorseful monk had prayed, it was found to be full of oil! And it was not only full, but even overflowed its brim, so that abundant streams of fine oil flowed forth over the floor . . .

* * *

On one occasion, Benedict went forth to visit his sister, Scholastica.[16] As they sat together at a table, she asked him if he would spend the night there, continuing their edifying and salubrious conversation until dawn. Benedict, however, would not by any means agree to this. She then bowed her head in prayer. And when she raised her head again, immediately tempestuous thunder and lightning began to resound, as well as an unremitting deluge of rain! Indeed, so torrential was the downfall that Benedict could not possibly set foot outside her dwelling that night—despite the fact that hitherto the weather had been perfectly fine.

Thus Saint Scholastica, who poured out tears in her prayers, had transformed thereby the calm serenity of the sky into heavy rain. Upon perceiving this marvel, the man of God exclaimed to her reprovingly, "My sister, what is this thing that you have done?"

To this, his holy sibling replied:

> "O Brother, I beseeched thee stay,
> Yet thou, alas, didst answer 'Nay!'

---

[16] According to ancient tradition, Scholastica, Benedict's sister, also lived a monastic life, in a community of nuns located close to her brother's monastery. Gregory's version of the narrative states that it was the custom of Benedict to visit his sister once each year for spiritual conversation. Other sources indicate that Scholastica was a twin to Benedict, and that she (like Benedict) had commenced her religious life as a hermit, before becoming the leader of a convent. Her feast is observed on February 10, the date on which she died.

But I then to the Lord did turn,
To grant the boon for which I yearn.

"Now God himself hath sent this rain,
Thy pious self here to detain,
That thus thou'll tarry through the night,
And we may talk till morning's light!"

To this, she added jestingly, "Leave me now, good brother, if thou be able!" But, of course, due to the violence of the tempest and heaviness of the rain, Benedict had no choice but to stay. Thus it transpired that the brother and sister spent the entire night together, engaged in the delights of holy colloquy on the spiritual life, celestial realities, and the wonders of Heaven.

It happened that just three days afterwards, when Benedict had returned to his monastery, he saw a vision of the soul of his beloved sister ascending into Heaven in the form of a radiant, white dove. And, indeed it was found to be the case that Scholastica had then died. Benedict ordered her body to be taken to his own monastery at Monte Cassino, and buried there in the same tomb which he had made ready for himself.

* * *

Shortly after this, one night as the servant of God, Benedict, was gazing out through the window of his cell in prayer, he perceived a brilliant ray of light shining down through the pitchy opacity of the starless skies. And suddenly, it was as if he could see the whole world—or rather, the whole created cosmos—contained within the golden radiance of that single glowing beam!

And amongst the revelations contained within that glorious ray of light, he saw the soul of Germanus, the bishop of Capua, ascending into Heaven. And, indeed, later he was to learn that this same Germanus had, in fact, passed away at that very time.

During that same year, he foretold his own demise to several of the brothers. Precisely six days before his death, he ordered the tomb which he had prepared as his final resting place to be opened. Then he began to suffer from a fever, which grew steadily more severe each day. When the sixth day had arrived, he requested that he should be taken to the oratory. There, he was fortified by receiving the sacrament of the Body and Blood of the Lord. Supported by the hands of his disciples, the saint stood upright with his eyes raised longingly to Heaven. And with words of suppliant prayer, he gave forth his noble spirit unto God as he breathed his last.[17]

Now on the same day on which the man of God had left this terrestrial realm and passed over to Christ, two monks received precisely the same revelation. These two brethren were in locations far removed from each other—one was alone in his cell, while the other was some considerable distance from the monastery. Both saw a glowing and luminous

---

[17] According to ancient traditions, the day on which Benedict died was March 21, and a Holy Saturday, i.e. the day before Easter Sunday. It was then about forty days after he had spent the night in holy conversation with his sister, Scholastica.

pathway, strewn with cloth-of-gold and innumerable, radiant lamps. This led from the cell of Saint Benedict upwards
to the Heavens.

And a certain man of venerable appearance appeared
before them and asked the monks, "To whom does this pathway belong?" When each of the monks confessed that they
did not know, the man said to them, "This is the pathway
prepared for Saint Benedict, by which that noble servant of
God even now ascends to the glory of Heaven!"

Benedict was buried in the oratory of Saint John the Baptist
at Monte Cassino, at the place where there had formerly
been a temple of Apollo, which the saint had destroyed.

CHAPTER 3

THE ORIGIN AND PROGRESS OF THE ORDER OF SAINT BENEDICT

Editor's Note: *The following description of the origins and progress of the Order of Saint Benedict is taken from* De Viribus Illustribus Ordinis Sancti Benedicti,[18] *written by Johannes Trithemius in the last decade of the 15ᵗʰ century. Trithemius was a Benedictine monk and served as abbot of the monastery of Sponheim in Germany and spiritual advisor to the Holy Roman Emperor. As well as being a diligent scholar of monastic and ecclesiastical history, he was also a talented mathematician and cryptographer, and regarded as the most learned man of his time. He provides a number of additional historical facts of the life of Saint Benedict which are not included in the biography written by Saint Gregory the Great, but based on widespread and trusted traditions. He also provides an overview of the saints, popes, and illustrious authors of the Benedictine Order. Some of the details*

---

[18] *Illustrious Person of the Order of Saint Benedict.*

Trithemius includes which relate very specifically to reforms and challenges in monasteries in his own times in Germany have been omitted.

1.
THE FOUNDATION OF
THE ORDER OF ST. BENEDICT

In considering the beginnings of our noble and ancient order, we shall commence from the person who first gave to us the institutes or Holy Rule of our monastic observance.

Benedict, who bequeathed to our orders its name of blessedness,[19] was the founder of our order. It was Benedict who gave to us the norm of religious living in coenobiums,[20] and who was the father and leader of the monks [of our order] since the beginning. He was born in the province of Norcia, and from illustrious parents shone forth himself as an illustrious man. His father, Probus[21], was the nephew of the Emperor Justinian and the count of Norcia. His mother, called Abundantia, was the marchioness of Monteferrante. Her life was imperiled whilst giving birth, but she brought forth twins—a son, Benedict, and a daughter by the name of Scholastica. Both

---

[19] *Benedictus* means "blessed" in Latin.

[20] A specific arrangement of cells.

[21] The name of St. Benedict's father is given by most sources as Eupropius, or sometime Eutropius. This name is from the Greek language, and means 'well directed.' It seems that Trithemius has here substituted a Latin name with an approximately equivalent significance ('Probus', meaning 'upright, virtuous.')

of these preferred the love of God to the things of this world, and both served the Lord in monastic life.

When Benedict was still a small boy, he was sent to Rome to pursue his studies, while his sister remained in the household of her father.[22] The boy Benedict, in Rome undertaking literary studies, perceived many to enter into death through the pitfall of vice. Therefore, he abandoned his studies and disdained the philosophies of this world. Called by the spirit of God and desiring to serve God alone, he sought for a place of solitude.

After living in solitude and practicing penances for many years, he emerged from the experience of a truly holy and perfected man. He then established many monasteries, and in these, he provided his monks with a rule of life. It is according to this rule that we [Benedictines] still profess to live until the current time, according to our capacities.

Benedict constructed a monastery at Monte Cassino, in the location of an ancient temple and altar dedicated to Apollo. He purged this place from all the impurity of the devil and converted it into a suitable habitation for monks. In this monastery at Monte Cassino, he served as abbot for thirty-four years. He also wrote there his rule, which is distinguished by discretion and clarity and elegance of expression.

His order spread to many parts of the world, even while he still lived. When many Catholic princes and devout prelates

---

[22] A widespread tradition holds that Benedict's mother died very shortly after giving birth to Benedict and Scholastica (or even during the birth).

of the Church heard of the most holy life of St. Benedict, they earnestly wished to establish monasteries following his rule in their own provinces and regions. Thus, the outgrowths of Benedict's [form of monastic life] spread as far as the sea, and its offshoots extended to far distant lands. For he labored not only for his own sake, but for the benefit of all those who sought the truth.

As far as the character and person of St. Benedict is concerned, he was firm in faith, strong in hope, and fervent in two-fold charity [that is, love of God and love of neighbor]. He was pure in mind and committed in his devotion. In prayer, he was ardent, and in meditation, he was inspired. In the reading of Sacred Scripture, he was sedulous and exalted in his contemplation. So that I may conclude this description briefly, he was distinguished by the ornament of all the virtues—humble, modest, sober, chaste, and quiet. If you wish to know both his interior and his exterior mode of life and conversion, you may simply read the rule which he wrote. For this holy man, who merited even to receive the gift of prophecy, was never able to live in any other manner than that which he preached to his own disciples.

As far as his exterior life is concerned, he was a perfect example, which blazed like a fiery beacon for all. He was humble, charitable, kindly, merciful, and a most vigilant shepherd to all the sheep of Christ. He preferred nothing whatsoever to the love of God. Nevertheless, when reason demanded it, he could be zealous and strict in discipline, for he constantly sought to refute and correct all perversity of life. If anyone wishes to know the story of Benedict's life, his mode of living, and his marvelous deeds more fully, they may read the second book of the *Dialogues* of blessed Pope Gregory.

This Benedict, the law-giver of our order, was born in the year of our Lord 480. He commenced his life in religious at the age of fourteen. He died in the year 542, at the age of sixty-three.[23] He was buried in the Church of St. Martin, which he had raised up in the same monastery at Monte Cassino. And it is from him that our congregation received the name of the Order of St. Benedict, as well our rule of life, known as the Rule of St. Benedict.

2.
THE PROGRESS AND SPREAD OF THE ORDER, AND THE FOUNDATION OF THE FIRST MONASTERIES

The newly established Order of St. Benedict began to multiply and to extend itself into the most distant provinces of the earth. For, as we have said, whilst our holy father was still living, nobles of the earth and bishops of the Church from remote regions sent delegates to him, postulating that he send brethren to them to act as teachers and leaders of his form of monastic life. For this, they requested monks who were suitable to teach and instruct others in Benedict's own manner life.

---

[23] Most scholars now believe that Benedict died in 547.

Out of such monks who were thus sent forth to found new monasteries, St. Maur was dispatched to Le Mans, upon the bishop of that place; he founded there a monastery and gathered to it a great many sons in Christ. Saint Placid, another disciple of Benedict, was directed to Sicily, where, after a number of years, he was made a martyr for Christ, together with some thirty other brethren.

After the death of our most blessed father, Benedict, the holy order continued to increase magnificently for almost six hundred years. And a vast number of monasteries were established, and amongst all other religious orders, the Benedictine held primacy in both number and merit.

Oh, how great was the devotion of the princes of ancient times to our order! How great was the solicitude of the bishops of the Church for the needs of our monks! Indeed, these applied all their efforts and resources to raising up new monasteries to the praise of God.

Thus, it is clear that our order, from the times of Benedict, flourished for many years. Indeed, it was the Benedictine Order which sustained the Church in praiseworthy fashion for many centuries. During these times, the brethren living in our monasteries not only were pre-eminent in sanctity of life, but they supported the evangelization of vast multitudes of peoples in many regions.

3.
SAINTS AND CANONIZED PERSONS FROM THE ORDER OF ST. BENEDICT

God, who is glorious in his saints, has adorned our order from its beginning with many most holy men and women. These saints have shone forth in their sanctity of life and virtue, as is shown clearly in the writings of their lives and deeds. And is it any wonder that the Order of St. Benedict has been shone with so many luminaries, since it has endured for such a great length of time? For our order flourished for seven centuries, and during this time has never been without its own illustrious men and women. Indeed, it would be impossible for us even to list only the names of all the saints of the order. The number is so vast, that to many it would appear almost incredible.

And so that due reverence were given for such a compendium [of Benedictine saints, were it ever to be written], a sense of the magnitude of the totality of the illustrious men and women of our order may be demonstrated by a few observations. In the days of Pope John XXII,[24] out of the annals of the popes and old histories, a catalogue of the names of the saints of the Benedictine Order was compiled, including both simple monks and nuns, and those who had been raised to the episcopy and other ecclesiastical dignities. It contained the names of some 15,559 saints! Who could possibly make mention of all of these?

---

[24] John XXII occupied the papacy from 1316 to 1334.

Rejoice, O Father Benedict! For you have led so many souls to Christ the King, by means of your most holy rule and institutions, such that no other order may presume to equal you in sheer numbers. Now, exulting with the angels in the Heavenly kingdom, in prophetic words and applause you may testify, "Behold, it is I and the children whom the Lord has given me!"[25]

4.
POPES, CARDINALS, ARCHBISHOPS, AND BISHOPS FROM OUR ORDER

It is a true sentence of the Lord, and one which is fulfilled in our own order, which declares that, "A city positioned on a mountain is not able to be concealed; and no-one lights a lamp that they may place it under a basket, but rather they place it on a lampstand so that it may illuminate all entering the house."[26] The Order of St. Benedict has not been hidden under a basket of abjection or oblivion. Rather, it has been exalted upon the lampstand of the Church, in order to offer the light of doctrine and sanctity to the faithful. Hence from its very beginning, the order has deserved to be greatly exalted in the Church of God. Thus from the flock of our Holy Father, St. Benedict, a Church has chosen a vast many priests and bishops[27] for

---

[25] Isaiah 8:18.
[26] Matthew 5:14-16.
[27] The Latin "*sacerdotes*" has been rendered as 'priests and bishops,'

itself. Indeed, which church would not wish, with the most fervent desires, to obtain for itself a pastor from the order of our Holy Father? For in this order, the love of the Christian religion has flourished, the light of sacred learning has beamed forth, and irreproachable uprightness of morals has shone brightly.

And so, it has come to pass that many brothers of this order have been called to diverse ecclesiastical dignities. Some, on account of their exemplary sanctity; others, because of the excellence of their sacred doctrine; others, from their tireless industry in achieving needed results; and yet others, because of their singular personal nobility. But all such persons [regardless of the diversity of their individual merits] have one important attribute in common: namely, the discipline of a life lived according to the monastic rule. Indeed, the love of the monastic life has provided priests and bishops for the people in a most marvelous manner.

From this most holy Order of St. Benedict, there have been some eighteen pontiffs of the Roman and universal Church. And these Benedictine popes, serving at different stages of history, have contributed magnificently to the expansion of the order. The order has also produced countless cardinals, archbishops, and bishops.

---

since that is the evident sense here.

5.
THE WRITERS AND TEACHERS OF OUR ORDER AND THE WONDROUS STUDIES OF THE MONKS OF OLD

From the beginning of our order, many most learned persons flourished in our order. For when St. Benedict was still living and the order had spread through different areas, many noble and learned youths resolved to submit themselves to living under his system of monastic life. These were not only most expert in the sacred writings, but equally erudite in secular studies.

One such person was the senator Cassiodorus, an extremely learned man, who renounced his senatorial dignity and become a monk, inspired by the love of God. As times passed, the work of scriptoriums was cultivated with the highest industry by monks, and a constant love of learning in all the good arts and fields of learning prevailed. The well-educated persons who were converted to monastic life served the junior brethren usefully by teaching them and instructing them.

Neither was youngness in years an impediment to the desire for progress in learning, since it was governed and directed by wise masters. So that we may offer a few examples from many, we call to mind Saint Boniface and Blessed Rabanus Maurus, both archbishops of Mainz, as well as Saint Bede the Venerable, an English priest. When Boniface was still a boy of five years of age, he was enrolled in a monastery in England, and from the very beginning excelled in his zealous studies of scripture, to such an extent that he came to be the teacher and apostle of the Germans. Various elegant letters which he addressed to various people have survived, and other writings. These writings overflow with his genius and with sacred doctrine.

Rabanus Maurus, who was sixth in succession as archbishop of Mainz after Boniface, come to conversion as a boy in the monastery of Fulda. The almost endless volumes which he composed demonstrate his proficiency in sacred knowledge. And he was expert not only in the sacred scriptures, but in virtually all humane studies. His marvelous work *De Laudibus Sanctae Crucis*[28] exhibits his powers as a poet. His expertise in the ancient histories is revealed in his great work *On the Universe.* And his mastery of the art of rhetoric shines forth copiously in his letters and other writings.

The Venerable Bede, a monk and priest who is known throughout the world, was entrusted to a monastery by his parents at the age of seven. His works are extolled with the highest praise throughout the universal Church.

These most holy men, expert teachers of the scriptures, learnt all that they came to know whilst living in monasteries under the rule of our order. They were not sent away to

---

[28] *Praises of the Holy Cross.* This remarkable work presents a set of mystical poems set out in complex diagrammatic form. It was in a manuscript containing this work which the details of the design and meaning of the medal or cross of Saint Benedict were discovered. See chapter 5.

foreign nations for the cause of their studies, since in their own monasteries they always had instructors in the good arts. There are many most erudite persons who entered monasteries during their youth and have shone forth gloriously both in their sanctity and learning, of whom I shall not make individual mention. For such persons, their love of learning and diligence adequately compensated for whatever deficiencies they may have had due to the youthfulness of their years.

We read of the many holy fathers of our order, and much is offered thereby for our imitation. Immense devotion burned within their hearts, and ardent zeal for disciplined observance of the rule flourished in their minds. This zeal prevented them from ever wasting their time in fruitless leisure. Apart from the praying of the divine office, the rest of their time was devoted to the study of holy writings. For by such study, not only is the intellect illuminated, but feelings are also moved to compunction. In this holy exercise of monks and nuns, love always sprang up, which called them to studious reading and vigilance in prayer. Those who devoted their attentions to reading of the sacred texts, would, in their free hours, apply themselves to writing commentaries and expositions of the same texts. Thus they produced books and treatises which encouraged the efforts and intentions of their brethren to seek after God.

But, in accordance with the rule, the other monks who were not capable of composing books did not give themselves over to idleness. Rather, after prayer, they gave themselves over to the manual work of copying books by hand. They copied books written by learned persons, which were apt for their times, and thus, from the original manuscripts, made these works available to the world. Others worked skillfully in the binding of volumes, others made corrections to copies, while others decorated volumes by rubrication.[29] There was no hand of any monk which did not participate in the work of producing books in some way! And all rejoiced to be participants in this endeavor. For, by this means, the junior monks were introduced to the scholastic disciplines, in a form and manner suited to each one. Some would apply themselves to grammar, while others would study orthography. There were those who learnt rhetoric, and others who mastered dialectics. There were monks who studied music, or arithmetic, or the art of computation; and yet others who studied philosophy. Once thoroughly grounded in such disciplines, they were then introduced to more speculative and contemplative writings. In our monasteries, no place was given to unproductive idleness, but rather, each monk applied himself to his own studies and labors.

6.
THE MIRACULOUS PROGRESS OF OUR ORDER IN EARLIER TIMES

The holy studies of the monks of early times earned for the order great devotion from both princes and the people.

---

[29] That is, by the application of red coloration to portions of the text. During the Middle Ages, it was a specialized craft.

With the help of these, our order made miraculous progress and attained to great heights. With nobles and rulers of the earth witnessing the holy manner of life of our monks, they granted many benefits and resources to our monasteries. By means of these gifts and donations, our monks were able to remain quietly and securely in their service of God. Some benefactors raised up monasteries of our order from their own properties and endowed them magnificently out of their resources. Others donated enriched and expanded already-founded monasteries with generous gifts. Each and every one of them rejoiced to have made a contribution to our monks, to the glory of God and the honor of St. Benedict.

And as much as the monks of our order fervently loved the things of heaven, so much more did they prosper and increase in the resources of this world, as the devotion of the people towards them grew ever warmer and more affectionate. They loved God, and [in doing so] they possessed all things. Because they disdained the passing riches of this world, Christ provided for them all that was necessary. This is indeed what is spoken of in the Gospel, when it counsels, "Seek first the Kingdom of God and its righteousness; and all other things will be added to you."[30]

---

[30] Matthew 6:33.

CHAPTER 4

THE DESIGN AND MEANING OF THE MEDAL OR CROSS OF SAINT BENEDICT

The medal (or cross) of Saint Benedict has a remarkable and complex design, which is of great power and striking beauty. It is pertinent to note that the terms "medal" and "cross" may be used interchangeably—for this devotional object comprises an image of a *cross,* normally depicted upon a *medal.* Indeed, the papal brief granting official approval to its use explicitly notes that these objects of devotion are popularly known by a variety of names: *numismata seu medallias, vel cruces, aut cruculas* ("medals or medallions, or crosses, or small crosses").

It is to be noted that if the image or design of the medal (given below) is depicted or printed upon another object than a medal (and this practice is perfectly permissible), then obviously the term "cross of Saint Benedict" would be more appropriate than "medal of Saint Benedict."

The medal of Saint Benedict typically bears a design upon both its front and back. These are shown below.

Figure 1: Medal of Saint Benedict (front).

Figure 2: Medal of Saint Benedict (back).

This may be considered the "official" design, as defined by the description of the medal in the papal brief giving it official approval. In that document (which is included in full in chapter 8 of this volume), it is stated that:

> One side displays the image of Saint Benedict, and the other side has a cross, with these following letters or characters around its extreme edges:
>
> **V.** *Vade.* **R.** *retro.* **S.** *Sathana.* **N.** *numquam.* **S.** *suade.* **M.** *mihi.* **V.** *vana.*
> **S**. *sunt.* **M.** *mala.* **Q.** *quae.* **L.** *libas.* **I.** *ipse.* **V.** *venena.* **B.** *bibas.*
>
> On the vertical line of the cross are the letters:
>
>   **C.** *crux.* **S.** *sacra.* **S.** *sit.* **M.** *mihi.* **L.** *lux.*
>
> On the horizontal line of the cross are the letters:
>
>   **N.** *non.* **D.** *draco.* **S.** *sit.* **M.** *mihi.* **D.** *dux.*
>
> Finally, in the four corners are the letters:
>
>   **C.** *crux.* **S.** *Sancti.* **P.** *Patris.* **B.** *Benedicti.*

It is interesting that the designation of one side as the "front" and the other side as the "back" (as is commonly used today) is not contained in the official description. Indeed, it is the elements on the "back" which contain the most distinctive, complex, rich, and time-honored content of the sacred emblem.

It is also to be noted that a degree of artistic and individual variation is permissible in the medal, provided it conforms with the description given above. For this reason, there may be small differences in the precise appearance of one medal to another. These small differences in appearance and design (including color or proportion) are perfectly legitimate, and in no way effect its efficacy, power, or validity—provided that all the essential elements, as defined in the papal brief quoted above, are present. Medals may also legitimately include inscriptions or symbols identifying when and where they were made, and other elements of devotion. Common examples of these include the Latin word pax, meaning "peace," or the Christogram "IHS." (This may be seen in Figure 2)

One commonly encountered and very powerful additional devotional element is a short prayer for the assistance of Saint Benedict in the hour of death, inscribed around the circumference of the side containing the image of the saint. This is seen in the following example:

*Figure 3: Front of medal of Saint Benedict issued by
the Abbey of Monte Cassino, in 1880.*

The prayer around the circumference reads:

Ejus in obitu n[ost]ro presentia muniamur.
("May we be protected by his presence in our death.")

This verse is taken from a popular prayer to Saint Benedict for a happy death. The custom of adding it to the design immediately became prevalent after the special issue in 1880 by the Abbey of Monte Cassino of a medal which included this text (as shown in Figure 3). This medal was issued with papal approval, as a commemoration of the 1,400th anniversary of the birth of the Holy Patriarch of Monks (who was born in 480).

Interestingly, in earlier times, the medal did not usually display the image of Saint Benedict. The earliest references to the use of the medal (dating to the mid-1600s) make note of the cross and letters contained upon it, but do not make mention of an image of Saint Benedict. And in a publication dating from 1695 (*Traité des supersitions*[31] by Abbé Jean-Baptiste Thiers), the following illustration is given, which reflected designs that were in use at the time:

Figure 4: An early design of the medal of Saint Benedict.

---

[31] Treatise on Superstitions. Abbé Thiers includes the medal in his treatise on superstitions not because of any objections to the power and efficacy of the devotional object in itself, but rather because of the fact that it was (in his times) often used by persons who had no idea of, or interest in, its true spiritual meaning, as if the letters in themselves functioned as a kind of quasi-magical charm.

Interestingly, in this particular design, the letters on the circumference are on the other side of the medal to the cross and its inscriptions (unlike the current practice, which places them all on the same side).

The inclusion of the image of the saint on the medal in Pope Benedict XIV's official and definitive description of it certainly strengthens or highlights the spiritual connection to the great Patriarch of Monks. It also reflects the fact that, by the time he was writing (in 1741), it had become a fairly standard practice. The omission of the image of the saint in the earlier versions may well have been due largely to the artistic and technical difficulties of engraving such a picture on a small metal object. Of course, in those days, medals would have been individually crafted objects, and therefore would have been very strongly influenced by the personal or local preferences (and abilities) of individual devotees or artisans.

It is obvious, in any case, that the most essential and characteristic elements of the medal of Saint Benedict are the various combinations of characters or letters which are inscribed upon it. These are all filled with mystical meaning, and it is from these meanings that the power and efficacy of the design arises.

Surprisingly, until the mid-17th century, by which time the medal was already in widespread devotional popular use in certain parts of Bavaria, the significance of these letters was shrouded in mystery. Indeed, it was not known even to any living Benedictine monks, much less other people who wore the medal. The fascinating story of how their won-derful meanings came to be discovered in a centuries-old manuscript is included in the next chapter.

* * *

The various short Latin verses which these letters on the medal of Saint Benedict represent are given below, followed by an English translation of each.

Crux **S**ancti **P**atris **B**enedicti
Cross of [our] Holy Father Benedict.

Crux **S**acra **S**it **M**ihi **L**ux.
May the Holy Cross be light to me.

Non **D**raco **S**it **M**ihi **D**ux.
May the Dragon not be a leader to me.

Vade **R**etro **S**athana **N**umquam **S**uade **M**ihi **V**ana.
Get behind me, Satan: Never persuade me
[to do] vain things.

Sunt **M**ala **Q**uae **L**ibas **I**pse **V**enena **B**ibas.
What you like is evil; May you yourself
drink [your] venom!

It is pertinent to note that the Latin verses are written in poetic form, and in fact, exhibit very strong rhymes.[32] The

---

[32] The significance of the particular poetic form used in the Latin text (which are technically known as "leonine verses," or internally-rhymed hexameters) in establishing the antiquity of the medal of Saint Benedict will be discussed in the following chapter.

rhyming elements are highlighted below, by presenting the texts in question as couplets. In each case, the rhyming syllables are underlined:

> *Crux sacra <u>sit mihi lux.</u>*
> *Non draco <u>sit mihi dux.</u>*
> *Vade retro Sa<u>thana</u>;*
> *Numquam suade mihi <u>vana</u>.*
> *Sunt mala quae <u>libas</u>;*
> *Ipse venena <u>bibas.</u>*

English renditions of each of the above verses, exhibiting similar properties of rhyme, may be proposed. It is to be noted that, to achieve the desired rhymes, a high degree of literary liberty and paraphrase has been exercised.

> *Crux sacra sit mihi lux.*
> *Non draco sit mihi dux.*
> May the cross shine bright upon me:
> May the dragon stay far from me!
> *Vade retro Sathana;*
> *Numquam suade mihi vana.*
> O Satan, get behind me;
> To evil, never bind me!
> *Sunt mala quae libas;*
> *Ipse venena bibas.*
> Wicked things you love and think:
> Your own venom may your drink!

CHAPTER 5

THE REVELATION OF THE SPIRITUAL POTENCY AND MYSTICAL SIGNIFICATIONS OF THE MEDAL

Editor's note: *It is impossible to identify exactly when the medal of Saint Benedict first came into use, but its coming to the general attention of the Catholic faithful can be linked with certainty to particular dramatic events which took place in Bavaria in 1647. These events are described in the book* Benedictus Redivivus,[33] *by Fr. Gabriel Bucelin, OSB. Bucelin was the prior of the Imperial Benedictine Abbey of Saint John the Baptist in Switzerland, and a distinguished scholar, historian, and theologian.* Benedictus Redivivus, *published in 1679, is his masterpiece and enjoyed a wide circulation. It furnishes a detailed chronological account of the various signs and manifestations of renewal of the Order of Saint Benedict and Benedictine spirituality in Europe (especially in Germany), following the turmoil and violence of*

---

[33] *Benedict Revived.*

the Protestant schism. He considered emergence of widespread use of the medal of Saint Benedict as an important element in the revival of popular devotion and veneration to the great saint.

A translation of the passage in Bucelin's book in which he described the events of 1647 is provided below:

In the Year of Our Lord 1647, the cross of Saint Benedict, which was by then already in widespread use and had been revered for some centuries, began to shine forth with a new and radiant splendor. This came about in the following manner.

In a certain town [in Bavaria] called Natternberg,[34] a coven of wizards and witches had been discovered. Once these vile and viper-like malefactors were arrested by the authorities, they were placed in chains and carefully questioned as to their nefarious activities and practices. In the course of their confessions, they revealed that their black arts were utterly powerless wherever they encountered a particular type of cross or medal [i.e. that of Saint Benedict.] For, wherever it was painted or engraved, it served as an invincible shield against the forces of evil which they employed.

They went on to say that they had found that their works had no effect in the monastery at Metten[35] in Bavaria, for many such crosses were located there. Once he had heard of this, the magistrate [of Natternberg] betook himself to the holy

---

[34] A village in Deggendorf, in Lower Bavaria.
[35] A town in Lower Bavaria, which sprang up around the Benedictine monastery which was founded there in 766. It is about two miles from Natternberg.

[Benedictine] fathers at Metten. The monks [knew about the special crosses, which were kept in their monastery, and used as sacred emblems by people in the area, but they] knew nothing of the meaning of the letters which were written upon them.

However, they investigated carefully, and at last certain monks of the monastery chanced to find an ancient manuscript in praise of the holy cross, in which the mystery of the letters inscribed upon this medal were fully explained. Now, even if the book had been decorated with gold and precious gems, it would still be more precious on account of the various relics of saints and holy objects which were inserted into it.[36] It was dispatched at once to Ingolstadt, and from thence to Munich where it was shown to the Most Serene Elector, [the Duke of Bavaria.]

Editor's note: *It is to be noted that this narrative, though the most frequently cited, was not the very earliest published account. An anonymous pamphlet or booklet, entitled* Les effets des vertus de la croix ou médaille du grand patriarche saint Benoit,[37] *also describes the events which took place in 1647. It was published in Paris in 1668, scarcely two decades after the time in question. The account it offers is slightly more detailed and complete than that offered in Benedictus Redivivus, but entirely consistent with it. Interestingly, it contains an illustra-*

---

[36] Details of the holy relics contained in this manuscript volume will be given a little later in this chapter.

[37] *The effects of the virtues of the cross or medal of the great Patriarch, Saint Benedict.*

tion of the design of the medal identical to that shown in Figure 4. A translation of the relevant passage if given below:[38]

In the year 1647, when sorcerers were being hunted down in Bavaria, and when several had been executed in the town of Straubing, some of them, under interrogation, acknowledged to the judges that their sorcery had been unable to have its intended effect on persons or animals from the Castle of Natternberg, near the Benedictine Abbey of Metten, because of some sacred medals which were in the places they indicated. These were in fact found there, but no one, not even the sorcerers themselves, could decipher the characters they had engraved on them. However, finally an ancient manuscript was discovered in the library of that Abbey which gave a perfect clarification of their meaning.

All that had transpired was reported to the Duke of Bavaria. Wishing to inform himself accurately of this, he had the medals and the manuscript brought to the town of Ingolstadt, and from there to Munich, and having compared the two [i.e. the medals and the texts in the manuscript], he gave an assurance that these medals could be used fruitfully and legitimately, without the least suspicion of error or superstition. The Duke then had a written report of the proceedings prepared.

Editor's note: *One of the intriguing features in both of these accounts is the discovery of a certain ancient manuscript in the Benedictine Abbey of Metten, which elucidated the mystery of*

---

[38] The editor gratefully thanks Fr. David Barry, OSB, for his generous assistance in translating this passage.

the meaning of the letters inscribed upon the medal. Neither Bucelin, nor the earlier anonymous booklet, provide any specific information on this momentous manuscript. However, the details of this remarkable and important document were diligently recorded by the learned Dom Bernhard Pez, OSB, the librarian of Melk Abbey,[39] in the first volume of his Thesaurus Anecdotorum Novissimus,[40] published Augsburg in 1721. Below is a translation of the passage in question.

[In the Abbey of our order at Metten,] we examined carefully three volumes. Of these three, one was of the greatest importance, for it illuminated the question of the origin and meaning of the cross or medal of Saint Benedict. This cross or medal is truly a most potent protection or amulet against the deceptions of demons, the curses and malice of witches, and attacks of evil spirits. Indeed, a coven of sorcerers who had been arrested had admitted that all their hellish arts and diabolic devices were utterly powerless against this Abbey of Metten, because this mystical sigil—the cross of Saint Benedict—protected it so invincibly. When the official investigators followed up this confession, they discovered that there were indeed many such crosses displayed in various locations throughout the monastery. [Nevertheless, none of the monks knew the significance of the mysterious letters inscribed upon it.]

However, after a careful search, an ancient codex was found

---

[39] In Switzerland.
[40] *Treasury of Recent Discoveries.*

hidden away in an obscure and dusty corner of the monastery. And in this old and long-forgotten manuscript volume was found a most remarkable image of the Holy Patriarch which revealed in full those sacred and powerful words, the initials of which were displayed upon the cross of Saint Benedict! And we looked upon this very same precious codex, mindful of its momentous significance, and had the opportunity of examining carefully its contents. This was, for me, truly a most awe-inspiring and overwhelming experience. . . .

The manuscript volume, which is written on leaves of parchment and is of a large size, contains several works.[41] Firstly, there are the four Gospels. Secondly, there is the famous *Praises of the Holy Cross* by [Blessed] Rabanus Maurus. Thirdly, there is the *Biblia Mariana*,[42] attributed (by some) to Saint Albert the Great, which has illustrations of various figures from the Old and New Testament. Fourthly, there is a short series of illustrations with inscriptions. These were produced by the hand of an anonymous monk of the same Abbey of Metten, who lived in the 15th century during the time of the Abbot Peter. Among this series of illustrations is an image of Saint Benedict, bearing in his hand a cross [and banner]. And the holy words signified by the letters on the

---

[41] It was usual in manuscript volumes to include a number of different works. Sometimes these were thematically or historically related, but this was not necessarily the case.

[42] This work is an assembly of scriptural texts which seem to relate to the Blessed Virgin Mary.

medal of Saint Benedict (which were previously not known to any one) are written there in full!

Fifthly, the volume contains a listing of all the books of the Old and New Testaments; and sixthly, there is the *Compendium of the stories of the Old and New Testaments* by Peter of Poitiers.

At the very beginning of the codex is a description of the various holy relics which are contained within it.[43] It reads thus:

> The following sacred relics are hidden in this holy book: fragments from the crown of thorns of the Lord, the stone of the Lord,[44] the stable of the Lord, the stone on which the cross of Christ was raised,[45] the peas which were turned into stones,[46] the oil of Saint Mary [Magdalene,] the rod of Saint Peter, the cross of Saint Andrew [........][47]

---

[43] It was customary to have holy relics inserted into the binding of volumes which were especially important, in order to consecrate and protect them and bestow blessings upon those who read them. These relics would typically be extremely very small fragments or particles.

[44] This is a reference to the stone Christ prayed upon in the Garden of Gethsemane, and which was venerated in the Middle Ages as a most holy relic.

[45] According to ancient traditions, the stone in which the cross of Christ was affixed was the same as the very first stone which Solomon had ordered to be prepared for the ancient temple in Jerusalem, and which had stood in the center of that first temple.

[46] The editor has not been able to identify the meaning of this reference. It may pertain to a legend or tradition in circulation at the time.

[47] This list of holy relics continues at some length, and includes a large number of other saints.

Editor's note: *It was the illustration of Saint Benedict holding a cross (and banner), with the sacred verses represented by the letters on the medal of Saint Benedict (in the volume described above), which held the key to the revelation of their true meaning. The dating of this picture, given above by Pez simply as the 15th century, can be determined more precisely by a verse contained in the same codex, which specifies the year as 1415.*

The remarkable image of Saint Benedict, including the verses represented on his medal, is reproduced below.

Figure 5: Saint Benedict holding a cross and banner, displaying the verses represented by the letters on the medal, reproduced from an anonymous manuscript at the Abbey of Metten that was produced in 1415.

A careful examination of the image above shows that there is a slight difference in wording in one of the verses from that typically found on medals today. Instead of Ipse venena bibas *(which is the wording now generally accepted, and officially recognized in the document conferring papal approval on the medal), the illustration reads:* <u>Ipsa</u> venena bibas. *This earlier form (with* ipsa *rather than* ipse*) would give a very slightly different meaning: "What you like is evil: May you drink these venomous things!" In this interpretation,* ipsa *is functioning as a neuter plural accusative demonstrative pronoun, and is apparently implying "vices"* (vitia) *as the object. This interpretation is strongly supported by the illustration which immediately follows in the codex, which is a graphic representation of the seven capital vices. This illustration is reproduced below.*

Figure 6: A graphic representation of the seven capital vices, reproduced from the 1415 manuscript at the Abbey of Metten, and immediately following the illustration of Saint Benedict shown in Figure 5.

***

The work which immediately precedes this series of illustrations is the De Laudibus Sanctae Crucis[48] *by Blessed Rabanus Maurus. Rabanus Maurus (780-856) was a Benedictine monk, who became archbishop of Mainz. A man of legendary erudition, the* Laudibus Sanctae Crucis *is his literary and spiritual masterpiece. It presents a series of graphic poems of phenomenal complexity and genius. These focus on the sacred power of the form of the cross, as well as the mystical significance of inspired verses and the arrangement of letters which represent them. An example of one of the poems from this great work is given below.*

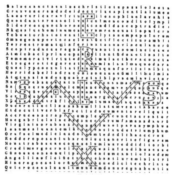

Figure 7: From De Laudibus Sanctae Crucis by Blessed Rabanus Maurus.

The text in large characters, CRUX SALUS, *means "The cross [is] salvation." Reading the small characters horizontally, one finds coherent sacred verses written in complex, highly literary Latin (on the nine orders of angels, in their veneration of the cross). But if the letters contained within the larger nine*

---

[48] *Praises of the Holy Cross.*

characters are the read separately, the names of the nine orders of angels are found! For example, the large letter L *in the center of the poem contains within it, in small letters, the word* Throni *("thrones"), and the large* A *to the left of this contains within it, in smaller letters, the word* Potestastes *("Powers").*

Another well-known example of graphic poetry drawing upon the power of the cross is the so-called Crux Angelica, *shown below (Figure 8). This graphic poem was produced by Venantius Fortunatus (530-610), the author of the celebrated Passiontide hymn* Vexilla Regis. *Fortunatus, who was born while Saint Benedict was still alive and active, was the official court poet of the Merovingian dynasty, and later became bishop of Poitiers. Interestingly, this ingenious creation is often mistakenly attributed to Saint Thomas Aquinas. It is, however, unquestionably the work of Fortunatus; but it seems that the Angelic Doctor had a great love and admiration for it, and made many copies of it for his own devotional use and spiritual protection.*

Figure 8: The Crux Angelica, *by Venantius Fortunatus, a contemporary of Saint Benedict.*

The four verses (shown at the sides of the cross) may be read in the letters, beginning with the central **C**, *and then progressing in any direction—upward, downwards, to the left, or to the right (and even changing direction as one reads!) The meaning of the verses are:*

> Crux mihi certa salus—*The cross [is] to me certain salvation.*
> Crux Domini mecum—*The cross of the Lord [be] with me.*
> Crux mihi refugium—*The cross [is] to me refuge.*
> Crux est quam semper adoro—*The cross is what I always adore.*

* * *

On the basis of the historical sources surveyed above, a number of conclusions may be confidently drawn regarding the antiquity of the medal of Saint Benedict. Firstly, it was the publicity attached to the dramatic events of 1647 that lead to the widespread dissemination of devotion to the medal of Saint Benedict. Secondly, despite this relatively late date for the popularization of the medal, it was already in popular devotional use in the area surrounding the Abbey of Metten by the mid-1600s. Furthermore, according to Bucelin, it had been venerated as a sacred emblem for some centuries prior to this time. Thirdly, the use of the medal of St. Benedict must already have been prevalent by 1415, when the illustration containing the verses which its letters represent (Figure 5) was produced.

A fourth conclusion may also be offered, arising from the nature of the verses themselves. In chapter 4 of this work, it was shown that the verses follow a clear pattern of rhyme. In fact, they also employ a particular type of meter, known as a "leonine verse" (or internally-rhymed hexameters). Without going into the technical details of Medieval prosody, this form of poetic meter was extremely popular from the 11th to the 13th centuries (although occasional earlier examples of it may be found). However, by the 14th and 15th centuries, it was no longer in general use, being considered archaic and crude by that time. On the basis of this fact, combined with the existence of the 1415 manuscript, it seems reasonable to hypothesize that the medal (or at least the verses represented by it) probably originated sometime during the 11th, 12th, or 13th centuries. Moreover, since its use was apparently confined to the Abbey of Metten and the surrounding region (at least until 1647), it seems reasonable to conclude that it originated in that area, and almost certainly from that particular monastery.

These conclusions, however, still leave a great many elements of uncertainty about the origin and early history of the medal of Saint Benedict. It may be that further discoveries in the libraries of the ancient Benedictine monasteries of Europe may shed further light on this fascinating mystery.

CHAPTER 6

DOCUMENTED POWERS OF THE MEDAL AND ITS MANNER OF USE

Editor's note: *The following is a translation of the description of the powers of the medal and its manner of use, contained in Benedictus Redivivus (1679) by Fr. Gabriel Bucelin. OSB. It is to be noted that he was recording only the powers and effects of the medal that had been observed in his own times, and the customs regarding use of the medal that prevailed when he was writing. Because of this, his descriptions should not be taken as being comprehensive, definitive, or authoritative. Nevertheless, they are quite fascinating in their own right, and there is no reason to doubt the accuracy and reliability of what he relates.*

The effects produced by the blessing and singularly potent protection of Saint Benedict which work through this holy medal, by the grace of divine mercy, have been frequently observed and clearly demonstrated a great many times. These are enumerated below.

1. The medal expels from human bodies any curses and compulsions induced by witchcraft, and all such works of the devil.
2. In any place where the medal is located, it prevents any warlock, wizard, or witch from entering.
3. Whenever the medal is present, it provides relief and remedy for all souls who are affected by spells or curses.
4. For any milk which has been cursed or affected by a spell or curse to prevent it from being successfully churned into butter, the presence of the medal entirely annuls the effect of such a spell or curse; so that the milk may successfully be churned into butter.[49]
5. The medal provides safety for all persons who are being vexed or attacked by demons or evil spirits of any kind.

Indeed, the medal of Saint Benedict is a powerful force in overturning all the effects of the diabolic arts, and also preventing any spells, illusions, curses, and other works of

---

[49] The special mention of this particular benefit of the medal may strike contemporary readers as unusual. However, in the 17th century, making butter from milk was an important part of daily domestic and economic life for many families, especially those in rural areas. It was believed that this process was very easily susceptible to the influence of spells and curses.

sorcery from gaining ascendency! It is a reliable source of strength and relief for those afflicted or tempted by evil spirits, and any other nefarious and occult influences. And it is a true fount of solace for those who are subject to the darkness of despair.

* * *

The method of using the medal is very simple. It may be worn around the neck [upon a chain or cord], or carried about, or worn upon one's person in some other convenient manner. The medal may also be placed in a vessel of water for a time, and the water will become imbued with its spiritual potency. This water may be given to animals to drink (or the animals washed with this water), in order to protect them against the effects of witchcraft, or to restore them from any such ill effects. The design of the medal may be positioned on doorposts, doorways, and fences, either by painting it or carving, to provide protection from evil spirits and to inhibit the entrance of sorcerers and witches.

All of the above modes of using the medal or cross should, of course, be done with firm faith in God and confidence in the singular merits of Saint Benedict. These, and countless other benefits, have been experienced as a result of this mystical sigil and are confirmed by the testimony of a great many devotees.

CHAPTER 7

VARIOUS MIRACLES PROCURED THROUGH THE MEDAL IN THE YEARS OF OUR LORD 1665 AND 1666

Editor's Note: *Over the centuries, a countless multitude of miracles have been experienced through the power of the medal of Saint Benedict—or rather, through the power of God responding to the intercession of the great saint, which is invoked by the presence and veneration of the medal. In Benedictus Redivivus, a series of some eleven striking miracles (all occurring in the years 1665 and 1666) are carefully recorded. These were all reliably recounted to Bucelin by credible eye-witnesses to the events, which were then still relatively recent. It is very clear from these narrations that the influence of evil spirits and witchcraft were of genuine concern to people at the time, and a real (and perilous) part of the daily fabric of life. A translation of the Latin text of Bucelin's account of these miracles is provided below:*

1.
A Demon is Expelled from a Possessed Man Through the Cross of Saint Benedict

In the year 1665, there was in Luxembourg a young man who was possessed by a devil, which tormented him very grievously. No remedy could be found for this possession, until the man was given to drink water in which a cross of Saint Benedict had been immersed. Immediately, after drinking a little, when he removed the goblet containing this water from his lips, the devil began to rage with unprecedent violence, tossing the man about and twisting his limbs horribly. At last, however, the devil was compelled to speak. The infernal spirit announced that he would depart from the body of the possessed man at the third hour of that night, since he could not tolerate the presence within the man's body of the water consecrated by the cross of Saint Benedict. The young man's parents heard this and were somewhat comforted, but not absolutely convinced of the truth of this promise. Nevertheless, at precisely the third hour of the night, the demon *did* depart from the young man, and he was restored to perfect health and sanity.

2.
A YOUNG GIRL WHO IS UNABLE TO CONTROL HER TONGUE IS CURED

In the same city of Luxembourg, there was a young girl who was unable to control the utterances of her tongue. This manifested itself in her saying indecent and obscene words and exclamations, apparently without any intention of doing so. It was concluded from this involuntary and disgusting type of speech that some form of impure spirit must have taken possession of her mouth and was able to assume control of it at certain moments. She was likewise given to drink some water in which the cross of Saint Benedict had been immersed. And—behold!—once she had drunk this consecrated liquid, she gained perfect control over her tongue! Never again did she utter obscenities, but rather henceforth all her words were perfectly consistent with Christian decency and modesty.

3.
A TORMENTED DEMONIAC IS LIBERATED FROM DIABOLICAL POSSESSION

In the town of Vesoul in Burgundy in France, there was a certain man who had long been possessed by a demon, which had tormented him terribly over many years. At last, the citizens held a meeting as to how to cure him, or (at least) to control and restrain him. At this gathering, a certain pious citizen suggested that the medal of Saint Benedict would offer a reliable remedy. So, a medal was procured and placed into a cup containing drink. This cup was then given to the possessed man to consume. This he did, and he was immediately liberated from possession. And never again was he troubled by the assaults of evil spirits.

4.
THE LIFE OF A WOMAN STRUGGLING IN CHILDBIRTH IS SPARED BY THE INFLUENCE OF THE MEDAL OF SAINT BENEDICT

In the month of April in the year 1666, in the town of Besançon [in eastern France], a certain pregnant woman was approaching the time of delivery of her child, and she began to experience the most horrendous pains. Despite her pangs of labor, she was not able to deliver her baby, but twisted and turned terribly and tortuously. The midwife and other women present were utterly unable to induce her to deliver the child or to relieve her pains. And despair fell over everyone, for it seemed quite certain that both the mother and child were destined to perish.

But at this point, Fr. Constantius Gravel, a priest of our order and the subprior of the Monastery of Saint Vincent at Besançon, was summoned to the bedside of the afflicted woman. He had with him a medal of Saint Benedict, which he carefully placed around her neck. Straightaway, the woman felt her pains begin to reduce in intensity. After Fr. Gravel had departed, within a very short space of time—no longer than it takes to say the fiftieth Psalm [the '*Miserere*']—she had delivered the infant! But, very sadly, it was dead. . . .

Nevertheless, the life of the mother was spared, all through the influence of the holy medal.

5.

MALIGN SPIRITS ARE EXPELLED FROM A HAUNTED CASTLE BY THE CROSS OF SAINT BENEDICT

About eight miles from the same town of Besançon, there is an ancient and abandoned castle or fortress, known as the Castle of Maillot. Now, this noble but decrepit edifice was haunted by a multitude of demons and malign spirits; and the people who resided in the area were all filled with fear of the ancient ruin and the eldritch entities that dwelt therein. For they would frequently hear hideous wailings and groans at night, and they were filled with a nameless horror at the diabolic influence which seemed to emanate from the place. Moreover, these ghosts or demons severely afflicted even the beasts who inhabited the area, with many unexplained instances of sickness and sudden death occurring.

There appeared to be no way of expelling the fiends and specters who haunted the castle, for all attempt at exorcism had been unsuccessful. But, in the year 1666, the local inhabitants decided to employ the mystical cross of Saint

Benedict to relieve them of their unwanted, ghostly neighbors. So the design of the cross was placed all around the abandoned castle. And very soon, the symptoms of haunting completely ceased. The troublesome spirits departed, the ancient ruin became quiet, and tranquility and peace was once more restored to the region.

6.
THE MEDAL OF SAINT BENEDICT HEALS A MAN OF A MYSTERIOUS WOUND CAUSED BY WITCHCRAFT

In the year 1665, there was a man whose arm became afflicted by a very severe wound, or abscess, of unknown origin. This wound was extremely large and immensely painful. No ointment, balm, nor bandage had any effect upon it, and the surgeon whom the man consulted (who was an experienced and skillful practitioner) was perplexed and bewildered. In frustration, he declared that it was utterly beyond his skill to heal his patient of this inexplicable ulcerous deformity.

Later, when the surgeon discussed the matter with a certain pious friend of his, that friend wisely suggested to him that he should try using the medal of Saint Benedict as a remedy for the wound. For, he reasoned, if the abscess has not responded to any natural or medical treatment, it must have a spiritual or occult origin—that is, it must be the result of some covert work of witchcraft or spell directed against the man. And, if this were the case, only a spiritual remedy, such as the medal of Saint Benedict, could have any positive effect.

The surgeon followed this prudent and sagacious advice. He affixed a cross of Saint Benedict directly to the man's wounded arm, holding it firmly in place with bandages. And the next day, when the bandage and cross were removed to examine the injury, a large dart or nail-like object came forth from the lacerated skin! This had certainly not been there previously, for the wound had been carefully examined many times; thus it was clearly nothing other than the product of the sorcerous maleficence of the black arts.

Immediately afterwards, the wound began to respond to conventional treatments, and very soon, it was healed completely.

7.
A GRAVELY ILL MAN IS HEALED THROUGH THE VIRTUES OF THE MEDAL OF SAINT BENEDICT

In the same Year of Our Lord 1665, there was another man who was gravely ill. Doctors were duly consulted, but were unable to diagnose the cause of his illness or to suggest a remedy. Eventually, all his friends and family came to resign themselves to his impending death, for the sickness appeared to be fatal. But the sick man himself was not prepared to succumb to despair, and so he sought instead for a spiritual remedy. Accordingly, he procured for himself a medal of Saint Benedict. This he soaked in water overnight, and then piously and reverently drank the liquid which had thus been imbued with mystical power. And, to the great surprise and wonder of all, he was very soon restored to perfect health!

8.
A VILLAGE AFFLICTED BY WITCHES WITH A SERIES OF FIRES IS SHIELDED FROM THEIR EVIL INFLUENCE BY THE MEDAL OF SAINT BENEDICT

In the year 1665, a certain village in Bavaria was most wretchedly afflicted by a coven of evil sorcerers who inhabited the region. For almost every day, a house in the village would catch fire, and it was found that these malignant fires were unextinguishable by any of the usual means. On the contrary, they would continue to burn fiercely and voraciously until the dwelling place had been utterly consumed. In this way, at least a dozen houses had been reduced to ashes. The tragic and devastating effect of this series of disasters on the locals may readily be imagined.

So, the villagers held a council. They resolved to approach a nearby Benedictine monastery, and there implore the holy monks for their spiritual assistance in protecting themselves against whatever evil forces were assailing them. This they did, and the abbot of the monastery gave the poor villagers a large number of crosses or medals of Saint Benedict. He advised them to place one upon the door of each house or building in the village; and so it was done.

And the spate of unexplained conflagrations immediately came to an end, and tranquility and safety was restored to the village once more. Evidently, the sacred emblems of the Holy Patriarch of Monks were more than sufficient to guard against the unhallowed powers of sorcery and witchcraft.

9.
DAIRY CATTLE IN BURGUNDY ARE CURED OF A STRANGE AFFLICTION BY THE CROSS OF SAINT BENEDICT

In the countryside of Burgundy, it happened that a great many dairy cattle were afflicted by a strange and hitherto unknown malady, which caused them to produce blood instead of milk. And many of the rural folk and farmers who encountered this problem found that the cross of Saint Benedict offered a sure remedy to this condition (whether it was a disease, a curse, or the effects of some evil spirit). It is superfluous to relate each and every case of this happening, for there were a great number of people who had very similar experiences; rather, it will suffice to describe one case as a typical example.

In the Year of Our Lord 1665, there was a certain innkeeper in rural Burgundy who owned a cow, which was normally a good provider of milk: however, it had contracted the afore-mentioned troublesome affliction, and for some four months gave forth blood rather than milk. Now, the innkeeper happened to hear of the efficacy of the cross of Saint Benedict in curing this unfortunate condition. So he procured one for himself, and immersed it in some water, leaving it to remain there for some time. Then he gave some of this consecrated water to his ailing cow to drink. And thereafter, the cow was restored to perfect health and gave forth pure and nourishing milk, just as it had done so reliably before.

10.
AN INFANT WHOSE LIFE IS IMPERILED IS RESTORED TO HEALTH BY THE MEDAL OF SAINT BENEDICT

There was once a small infant who had fallen prey to some grave illness. So strong was the hold of the sickness on the baby that he refused to accept any nourishment whatsoever, and he appeared to be heading very rapidly towards the grim threshold of death. Indeed, his parents were racked with despair, for their child's demise seemed inevitable. However, one of their relatives advised them to try applying the medal of Saint Benedict to the sick baby. Indeed, this relative had recently been given such a medal by a Benedictine priest, so he willingly gave it to the anxious parents. Without really expecting it to work, they placed the medal around the infant's neck. And, behold, the very next morning, they found that their young son had been restored to perfect health! Joyfully, they offered sincere thanks to their relative for his wise advice and unbounded gratitude to God and Saint Benedict, by whose virtues their beloved child was saved.

This took place in the Year of Our Lord 1666.

11.
THE EFFICACY OF A BRICKMAKER'S FURNACE IS RESTORED THROUGH THE VIRTUES OF THE MEDAL OF SAINT BENEDICT

There was a certain tradesman, whose craft and livelihood consisted of baking bricks and limestone blocks, which were then used for construction purposes. In his workshop, he had a large furnace, which he used for baking these materials. But it happened once that, however hot he made the fire within this furnace, it became incapable of cooking the bricks and blocks, and of bringing them to the requisite degree of hardness. As there was no physical nor natural explanation for this strange occurrence, the tradesman concluded that some ill-intentioned person, skilled in the necromantic arts, must have cast a spell upon his fire, or that some wicked and vexatious spirit had taken up residence in his workshop.

So, he procured a number of medals of Saint Benedict, and placed these in various locations on the walls of his workshop. After this had been done, the efficacy of the fires which he used for baking was immediately restored, and his bricks and blocks came out of the furnace perfectly cooked. Never again was his workshop troubled with evil spirits or the spells and curses of witches and warlocks, thanks to the presence of the medal of the Holy Patriarch of Monks.

CHAPTER 8

APPROVAL OF THE MEDAL BY THE HOLY SEE

Editor's note: *Like most devotions of a popular or localized origin, the medal or cross of Saint Benedict was already in wide use and its power and efficacy were generally understood by the faithful before it was granted formal or official approval by the Holy See. This approval was first conferred in 1741 by Pope Benedict XIV, who issued a brief on the medal or cross of Saint Benedict. In this document, he provides the wording of the "officially approved" blessing of the medal or cross. The brief also includes an extensive list of indulgences pertaining to those who wear or carry the medal and fulfill other requirements of prayer, devotion, or good works. A slightly abridged translation of this document is provided below. (All abridgements are noted).*

It is to be noted that even a medal which has not been blessed is not without its own efficacy. The particular requirements of blessing relate specifically to the obtaining of indulgences (as outlined below), whereas the properties and effects listed in chapter 6 (such the ability of the medal to protect against evil spirits and witchcraft) pertain to the design of the medal itself and are not dependent upon the specific requirements listed below.

For the perpetual memory of the thing. . .
At the most humble entreaties of Dom Benno Löbl, Abbot of the monastery of Brzewnow in Brauna, of the Order of Saint Benedict, Provost of Wahlstad in Silesia, mitred Prelate of the kingdom of Bohemia, and perpetual Visitor of the said Order of Saint Benedict in Bohemia, Moravia and Silesia: Our most Holy Father Pope Benedict XIV has graciously given and granted to the same Benno and to his successors (and also to all and each of the abbots, priors, and priests who for the time being are subject to him as Perpetual Visitator) the special faculty of blessing the medals known under the name of medals (or medallions, or crosses, or small crosses) of Saint Benedict.[50]

[The design of these medals is this:] One side displays the image of Saint Benedict, and the other side has a cross, with these following letters or characters around its extreme edges:

V. *Vade.* **R.** *retro.* **S.** *Sathana.* **N.** *numquam.* **S.** *suade.*
M. *mihi.* **V.** *vana.*
S.*sunt.* **M.** *mala.* **Q.** *quae.* **L.** *libas.* **I.** *ipse.*
V. *venena.* **B.** *bibas.*

---

[50] This restriction has since been removed. Under current Church regulations, medals of Saint Benedict may be legitimately blessed by any priest or deacon.

On the vertical line of the cross are the letters:

C. *crux.* **S.** *sacra.* **S.** *sit.* **M.** *mihi.* **L.** *lux.*

On the horizontal line of the cross are the letters:

N. *non.* **D.** *draco.* **S.** *sit.* **M.** *mihi.* **D.** *dux.*

Finally, in the four corners are the letters:

C. *crux.* **S.** *Sancti.* **P.** *Patris.* **B.** *Benedicti.*

The form of blessing to be used for the medals is as follows:[51]

V. Adjutorium nostrum in nomine Domini.
R. Qui fecit coelum et terram.

Exorcizo vos numismata, per Deum Patrem ✛ *omnipotentem, qui fecit coelum et terram, mare et omnia quae in eis sunt: omnis virtus adversarii, omnis exercitus diaboli, et omnis incursus, omni phantasma Sathanae eradicare et effugare ab his numismatibus, ut fiant omnibus, qui eis usuri sunt, salus mentis et corporis, in nomino Dei Patris* ✛ *omnipotentis, et Jesu Christi* ✛ *Filii ejus, Domini nostri, et Spiritus Sancti W Paracliti, et in charitate ejusdem Domini nostri Jesu Christi, qui venturus est judicare vivos et mortuos et saeculum per ignem. R. Amen.*
Kyrie eleison, Christe eleison, Kyrie eleison.
Pater noster, etc.
V. Et ne nos inducas in tentationem.
R. Sed libera nos a malo.

---

[51] The currently approved English form for blessing medals is included in the appendix.

V. Salvos fac servos tuos.

R. Deus meus, sperantes in te.

V. Esto nobis, Domine, turris fortitudinis.

R. A facie inimici.

V. Deus virtutem populo suo dabit.

R. Dominus benedicet populum suum in pace.

V. Mitte eis, Domine, auxilium de sancto.

R. Et de Sion tuere eos.

V. Domine, exaudi orationem meam.

R. Et clamor meus ad te veniat.

V. Dominus vobiscum.

R. Et cum Spiritu tuo.

Oremus.

Deus omnipotens, omnium bonorum largitor, supplices te rogamus, ut per intercessionem Sancti Patris Benedicti his sacris Numismatibus litteris et characteribus a te designatis tuam benedictionem ✠ infundas, ut omnes, qui ea gestaverint, ac bonis operibus intenti fuerint, sanitatem mentis et corporis, et gratiam sanctificationis, atque indulgentias nobis concessas consequi mereantur, omnesquo diaboli insidias et fraudes per auxilium misericordiae tuae effugere valeant, et in conspectu tuo sancti et immaculati appareant, Per Dominum, etc.

Oremus.

Domine Jesu, qui voluisti pro totius mundi redemptione de Virgine nasci, circumcidi, a Judaeis reprobari, Judae osculo tradi, vinculis alligari, spinis coronari, clavis perforari, inter latrones crucifigi, lancea vulnerari et tandem in cruce mori: per tuam sanctissimam Passionemque humiliter exoro, ut omnes diabolicas insidias et fraudes expellas ab eo, qui Nomen sanctum tuum his litteris et characteribus a te designatis devote invocaverit, it eum ad salutis portum perducere digneris, qui vivis et regnas, &c.

Benedictio Dei Patris ✠ *omnipotentis, et Filii* ✠*, et Spiritus* ✠ *Sancti descendat super haec Numismata, ac ea gestantes, et maneat semper: in nomine Patris* ✠ *et Filii* ✠ *et Spiritus* ✠ *Sancti. R. Amen.*

Being, therefore, desirous to enrich in a special manner, by spiritual favors and with the heavenly treasures of the Church, the aforesaid medals blessed by the Visitator (and the other Monks mentioned above) he [Pope Benedict XIV] has graciously given and granted to all and each of the faithful, of both sexes, who shall carry about their persons [or wear] one of these medals or crosses blessed in this manner, and shall at the same time perform the good works which are listed below in their respective places, the following indulgences, in the manner and form specified below:

Whoever shall regularly recite, at least once in the week, the Chaplet of our Lord, or that of the most blessed Virgin Mary, or the Rosary, or a third part of the Rosary [i.e. one mystery of the Rosary], or the Divine Office, or the Little Office of the most Blessed Virgin Mary, or the Office of the Dead, or the Seven Penitential Psalms, or the Gradual Psalms; or whoever shall regularly teach the rudiments of faith, or visit those who are in prison, or the sick in any hospital, or assist the poor, or either hear, or, if he is a priest, celebrate Mass; [and] if he is truly penitent and has confessed to a priest approved by the Ordinary, and has received the holy Sacrament of the Eucharist on any of the days following: namely the feasts of the Nativity of our Lord Jesus Christ, the Epiphany, Easter, Ascension, Pentecost, most Holy Trinity, and *Corpus Christi*; and on the feasts of the Blessed Virgin Mary's Conception, Nativity, Annunciation, Purification, and Assumption; and also on the first day of November, [that is] the feast of All Saints, and on the feast of Saint Benedict;[52] and [also] has devoutly prayed to God for the destruction of heresies and schisms, for the exaltation and propagation of the Catholic faith, for the peace and concord of Christian rulers, and for the other needs of the Roman Catholic Church, <u>he shall obtain a plenary indulgence and the remission of all his sins.</u>[53]

[Editor's note: *An extensive list of partial indulgences follows. For the sake of brevity, these have been omitted.]*

Whoever shall beseech God to spread and advance the Order of Saint Benedict shall become a partaker of all of the good works which in any manner whatsoever are done in the said order.

Whoever, being at the point of death, [while wearing, or carrying, a medal of Saint Benedict] shall devoutly commend

---

[52] July 11.
[53] This underlining is added by the translator.

his soul to God, and having previously gone to confession and received Holy Communion, if it is in his power to do so (or if not, having made from his heart an act of contrition), shall, with his lips (or, if he cannot do more, at least in his heart) invoke the names of JESUS and MARY <u>shall obtain a plenary indulgence and the remission of all his sins.</u>

Each person may gain for himself or apply (by manner of suffrage) to the faithful departed, the abovementioned indulgences, as also the remission of sins, and the relaxation of the punishments due for them.

Notwithstanding all things to the contrary, His Holiness has declared that the medals herein mentioned which have <u>not</u> been blessed by the monks aforesaid [of the Order of Saint Benedict], or by those to whom the Holy See has, by a special favor, granted the power, shall in no way obtain the above indulgences.[54] He also forbids that the said medals should be made of paper, or any similar material; and that unless they are made of gold, silver, brass, copper or other solid metal, they shall not gain any indulgences.

In all things relating to the distribution and use of the said medals, His Holiness orders that there should be observed the Decree of Alexander VII, of happy memory, published on the sixth day of February, 1657; namely, that medals which have been blessed and are therefore eligible to gain indulgences as here mentioned, cannot pass beyond the

---

[54] As noted, medals of Saint Benedict may now (according to current Church discipline) be legitimately blessed by any priest or deacon.

persons to whom they have first been given or for whom they have first been blessed; nor can they be lent, sold, or borrowed, without losing the indulgences which have been attached to them. If a medal is lost, another cannot be taken in its place [in respect to eligibility for indulgences] unless it has also been blessed, as described above; notwithstanding any concession or privilege to the contrary.

[**Editor's note:** *The concluding paragraphs then go on to specify that no priest, even if he is a bishop, who is not a monk of the Order of Saint Benedict should bless or distribute medals of Saint Benedict. It is pertinent to note, however, that the faculty of blessing medals of Saint Benedict has now been extended to all priests and deacons. Directions are then given for the publication of the decree.]*

Given at Rome, on the 23rd day of December, in the year 1741.
L. Cardinal Pico, Prefect.
A.M. Erba, Apostolic Protonotary, Secretary of the Sacred Congregation [for Indulgences].

A Prayer Based on the Verses in the Medal of Saint Benedict

O, Benedict, most holy,
Lead us by your light.
Let your strength and wisdom
Arm us for life's fight.

Let the cross shine brightly,
Lighting all our ways,
Let it ever guide us
Through our earthly days.

May the wicked dragon
Never be our guide,
For in his deceptions
Naught but evil hides.

Get behind me, Satan!
Lead me not to sin;

Vain are all your promptings:
My soul you'll never win!

Drink your own foul poisons,
Wicked lord of lies!
For each soul you capture
Perishes and dies.

May the holy medal
Of this mighty saint
Keep me in God's safety,
Clean from sin's foul taint.

Glory be to Jesus,
Heaven's holy King;
Ceaselessly, His praises
Shall His chosen sing!

Amen.

ENGLISH FORM FOR THE BLESSING OF MEDALS OF SAINT BENEDICT

Below is the currently approved English form of blessing for medals of Saint Benedict. This is similar in its basic outline to the Latin blessing approved by Pope Benedict XIV, and given in chapter 8. However, certain parts of the Latin form have been abridged or slightly modified in this English blessing.

V. Our help is in the name of the Lord.
R. Who made heaven and earth.

In the name of God the Father ✛ almighty, who made heaven and earth, the seas and all that is in them, I exorcise these medals against the power and attacks of the evil one. May all who use these medals devoutly be blessed with health of soul and body. In the name of the Father ✛ almighty, of the Son ✛ Jesus Christ our Lord, and of the Holy ✛ Spirit the Paraclete, and in the love of the same Lord Jesus Christ who will come on the last day to judge the living and the dead, and the world by fire. Amen.

Let us pray. Almighty God, the boundless source of all good things, we humbly ask that, through the intercession of Saint Benedict, you pour out your blessings ✠ upon these medals. May those who use them devoutly and earnestly strive to perform good works be blessed by you with health of soul and body, the grace of a holy life, and remission of the temporal punishment due to sin.

May they also with the help of your merciful love, resist the temptation of the evil one and strive to exercise true charity and justice toward all, so that one day they may appear sinless and holy in your sight. This we ask though Christ our Lord. Amen.

The medals are then sprinkled with holy water.

LIST AND SOURCES OF
FIGURES IN THIS WORK

A number of illustrations are included in this work, all of which are in the public domain. These are listed below, including details of their sources.

Figure 1: Medal of Saint Benedict (front).
Guéranger, Prosper. *Essai sur l'origine, la signification et les priviléges de la médaille ou croix de Saint Benoît. Poitiers: Oudin, 1862.*

Figure 2: Medal of Saint Benedict (back).
Guéranger, Prosper. *Essai sur l'origine, la signification et les priviléges de la médaille ou croix de Saint Benoît. Poitiers: Oudin, 1862.*

Figure 3: Front of medal of Saint Benedict issued by the Abbey of Monte Cassino, in 1880.
Medalla San Benito. Wikimedia Commons.

Figure 4: An early design of the medal of Saint Benedict.
Thiers, Jean-Baptiste. *Traité des supersitions.* Paris: Antoine Dezaillier, 1697.

Figure 5: Saint Benedict holding a cross and banner, displaying the verses represented by the letters on the medal, reproduced from an anonymous manuscript at the Abbey of Metten produced in 1415.

Pez, Bernhard. *Thesaurus anecdotorum novissimus.* Augsburg: Vieth, 1721.

Figure 6: A graphic representation of the seven capital vices, reproduced from the 1415 manuscript at the Abbey of Metten.

Pez, Bernhard. *Thesaurus anecdotorum novissimus.* Augsburg: Vieth, 1721.

Figure 7: From *De Laudibus Sanctae Crucis* by Blessed Rabanus Maurus.

Migne, J.P. (editor), *Patrologia Latina, Tomus CVII.* Paris: Migne, 1851.

Figure 8: The *Crux Angelica* by Venantius Fortunatus.

Thomas Aquinas. *Monita et Preces.* Wurzburg: Leo Woerl, 1882.